THE

SUPREMES'

GREATEST HITS

Michael G. Trachtman

Sterling Publishing Co., Inc.
New York

A John Boswell Associates Book

Design by Nan Jernigan

Library of Congress Cataloging-in-Publication Data Available
4 6 8 10 9 7 5 3

Published by Sterling Publishing Co., Inc.
387 Park Avenue South, New York, NY 10016
© 2006 by Sterling Publishing

Distributed in Canada by Sterling Publishing
c/o Canadian Manda Group, 165 Dufferin Street
Toronto, Ontario, Canada M6K 3H6
Distributed in the United Kingdom by GMC Distribution Services
Castle Place, 166 High Street, Lewes, East Sussex, England BN7 1XU
Distributed in Australia by Capricorn Link (Australia) Pty. Ltd.
P.O. Box 704, Windsor, NSW 2756, Australia

Printed in China
All rights reserved

Sterling ISBN-13:978-1-4027-4107-4
        ISBN-10: 1-4027-4107-3

For information about custom editions, special sales, premium and
corporate purchases, please contact Sterling Special Sales
Department at 800-805-5489 or specialsales@sterlingpub.com.

ACKNOWLEDGMENTS

It was John Boswell's idea that this book should be written, and that I should be the one to write it. I am incredibly grateful for his creativity and generosity, and for the help he has freely given me in my effort to fulfill his vision.

Lawyers sometimes forget how to write and think like non-lawyers. My wife, Jennie, provided invaluable simultaneous translation services as I struggled to overcome those disabilities. Many apologies to her and my son, Ben, for the attention paid to this manuscript at their expense, and many more thanks for their understanding and encouragement.

TABLE OF CONTENTS

Introduction

"A Government of Laws, Not Men"

High school civics students are taught that our system of government is comprised of three branches: the legislature makes the laws; the executive enforces the laws; and the courts interpret the laws. As for the Supreme Court, they know that it is the highest court in the land—the final word on legal disputes.

So far as it goes, all of this is true. But to describe the Supreme Court in this way is to describe champagne as grape juice, or the Grand Canyon as a river valley—accurate to a point, but so shallow and incomplete as to be grotesquely misleading. Over 150 years ago, de Tocqueville, the celebrated French political observer, studied the Supreme Court and concluded, "A more imposing judicial power was never constituted by any people." The same holds true today.

The Ultimate Check and Balance: "Judicial Review"

Like the highest courts of other democracies, the Supreme Court has the authority to decide, once and for all, what important laws really mean when applied to the real-life situations that arise after the laws are enacted. Does the Civil Rights Act of 1964 protect women against sexual harassment?

Does the Americans with Disabilities Act cover people with certain heart conditions? Various lower courts disagreed. The Supreme Court interpreted the wording and intent of the statutes, and made a ruling. End of controversy.

But the most momentous role the Supreme Court plays in our society extends well beyond interpreting statutes: the Supreme Court serves as the ultimate interpreter and protector of our most fundamental rights—the rights set forth in the Constitution. Most historians agree that the American Constitution is the oldest national constitution still in effect, and it has stood the test of time for a reason. The framers of the Constitution drafted a document that was definitive in many respects, but also sufficiently vague so that it could be applied to unimaginable, changing circumstances. The framers of the Constitution knew things would change as, of course, they did—no one could have anticipated the industrial revolution, or the aftermath of slavery, or World War II, or the Internet. They needed a mechanism to breathe continuing life into the Constitution. They needed, and therefore created, the Supreme Court.

The Supreme Court keeps the Constitution alive in two, related ways. First, in the same way it interprets statutes, it interprets the Constitution. Does the First Amendment right of free speech allow you to burn the flag as a political statement? Does the Constitution's "Commerce Clause" allow Congress to outlaw racial discrimination, or Internet pornography? Supreme Court justices decide these issues, and the myriad of other questions that define our rights and lifestyles, through a process that is both rooted in historical precedent, and at the same time highly intuitive and dependent on individual value judgments and philosophies. Through it all, the goal is to somehow determine what a group of eighteenth-century scholars, farmers, businessmen, soldiers, and politicians really meant by the words they wrote, and what they would have done if faced with a twenty-first century they could not have hoped to envision.

The second way the Supreme Court empowers the Constitution is what stupefied de Tocqueville, and so many others who have studied our democracy: the Supreme Court has the authority to decide that any act of a government official, and any law passed by a government body, violates the Constitution and is therefore invalid and of no effect. This power, termed the power of "judicial review," is virtually limitless. It encompasses the right to void the decisions of township officials, mayors, governors, and the president of the United States. It includes the right to strike from the books any township ordinance, state law, or Act of Congress. Supreme Court justices are appointed for life and, therefore, do not have to worry about making the popular decision, as opposed to the *right* decision. They can just say no.

This is a remarkable aspect of the American way of life. Through its proper exercise, the Supreme Court can ensure that it is the Constitution, not the people who happen to populate the Congress or the White House or the local city hall at any given time, which defines the extent to which our property and liberty can be compromised by our government.

This ultimate check and balance makes us what billions of people in the world strive to be—what John Adams first called a "government of laws, not men."

The Supreme Court has not been shy about using its authority. At times, the Supreme Court justices made decisions that were welcomed when they were handed down, but are now seen as horrifically wrong, and even repugnant.

At other times, they made decisions that were reviled, but are now seen as bastions of freedom and wisdom. Either way, it is difficult to overstate the influence the Supreme Court wields. The Supreme Court desegregated American schools. The Supreme Court allowed the internment of Japanese-Americans during World War II. The Supreme Court decided who you may, and may not, refuse to serve or hire in your restaurant or accounting firm. The Supreme Court decided what your rights will be if your employer sexually harasses you. The Supreme Court decreed and defined the right to an abortion. The Supreme Court decided how the forty-third president of the United States would be elected. The Supreme Court determined when your town council may appropriate your backyard and make it a parking lot for a shopping mall.

And it will be the Supreme Court that will resolve the hot-button issues of the twenty-first century. Will your school board be permitted to require your child to study "intelligent design" over your objection? To what extent will the federal government be permitted to monitor your emails and bank accounts in the name of national security? How far can we go in the effort to effectively limit the influence of corporate money in American elections? How will we deal with the myriad of issues, some known and many yet to be discovered, that the Internet and related technologies will present?

There is no appeal from a Supreme Court decision. It speaks last.

It is not surprising that the appointment of a Supreme Court justice stirs passions, argument and multimillion-dollar lobbying efforts—few persons in our society have more power to define how we live.

that no soldier shall be quartered in any house without the consent of the owner.

Fourth Amendment: This amendment protects the people against "unreasonable searches and seizures" by the government and requires that warrants be issued only on probable cause, and with specificity.

Fifth Amendment: This amendment provides a multitude of rights. It defines how certain indictments must issue. It protects people against "double jeopardy" (that is, being tried twice for the same crime). It provides the right against self-incrimination. It provides that persons may not be "deprived of life, liberty, or property, without due process of law." And it provides that private property may be taken by the government for public use, but that just compensation must be paid.

Sixth Amendment: This amendment provides criminal defendants with the right to a speedy and public trial by an impartial jury. It also provides a defendant with the right to be informed of the charges made, to confront the witnesses against him, to subpoena his own witnesses, and to have the assistance of counsel.

Seventh Amendment: This amendment provides for the right to a jury trial in certain civil cases.

Eighth Amendment: This amendment prohibits "cruel and unusual punishment" and forbids excessive bail and excessive fines.

Ninth Amendment: This amendment clarifies that although the Constitution provides certain rights to the people, it is not be interpreted as diminishing all of the other rights the people have under the law—in other words, the Constitution is not the only source of the people's rights.

Tenth Amendment: This amendment provides that all rights not delegated by the Constitution to the federal government are to be retained by the states or the people.

A great many Supreme Court cases focus on the effort to define and protect the rights of Americans as set forth in the Bill of Rights—and what to do when those rights conflict with one another. Several of those cases are discussed in the chapters that follow.

The Fourteenth Amendment

The Fourteenth Amendment to the Constitution was passed in 1868. It includes various sections, but the most renowned section includes the provisions known as the "Due Process Clause" and the "Equal Protection Clause," which guarantee basic freedoms that, like the Bill of Rights, have been continuing focal points for the Supreme Court: "No State shall make or enforce any law which shall abridge the privileges or immunities of citizens of the United States; nor shall any State deprive any person of life, liberty, or property, without due process of law; nor deny to any person within its jurisdiction the equal protection of the laws."

The specific wording of the Bill of Rights prohibited the federal government, but not the state governments, from compromising fundamental freedoms. The Fourteenth Amendment was enacted in the wake of the Emancipation Proclamation in order to make it clear that, at the very least, the states owed constitutional duties of due process and equal protection to all persons. Ultimately, the Fourteenth Amendment was interpreted by the Supreme Court to require that the states also respect the core provisions of the Bill of Rights, such as free speech, the free exercise of religion, the right to counsel, and so on.

Particularly in the twentieth century, the Supreme Court has addressed numerous issues arising from the reluctance of some states to comply with notions of due process and equal protection and to fairly apply the Bill of Rights. This has led to colossal societal changes, such as desegration, restrictions on the role of religion in schools and government, and the rights of the accused. Some of the most important of these cases are explained in the chapters that follow.

How the Supreme Court Works

The cases in this book illuminate how the Supreme Court has interpreted the Constitution and used its power of judicial review to define, and redefine, our way of life. To better understand how these cases came to be decided, it helps to understand what the Supreme Court is and how it goes about its business.

The Supreme Court is comprised of a chief justice and eight asssociate justices, all of whom are nominated by the president and confirmed with the "advice and consent" of the Senate. The senatorial confirmation process entails a detailed investigation, a lengthy Judiciary Committee hearing, and a full Senate vote. Particularly in the last twenty years, Senate confirmation has become a harrowing experience, drawing extensive television coverage and well-funded lobbying efforts reinforced by major media campaigns.

Presidents typically nominate someone they believe will share their political and judicial philosophies, but the history of the Supreme Court is replete with justices who were supposed to be of one stripe, and turned out to be much different. A lifetime appointment to a position with the power to change fundamental rights and national policies, free from direct political pressures, can easily change one's perspective and ideology.

President Eisenhower, for instance, appointed Chief Justice Warren, believing that he would be a conservative jurist. Warren turned out to be one of the most liberal and activist chief justices in history, prompting Eisenhower to call the appointment "the biggest damn fool mistake I ever made." When Justice Souter was nominated in 1990, the National Organization of Women, believing he would seek to overturn *Roe v. Wade*, distributed flyers blaring, "Stop Souter or Women Will Die." After he was confirmed, Justice Souter helped write the opinion reaffirming the continuing validity of *Roe v. Wade*.

In almost all instances, the Supreme Court gets to choose the cases it hears. After a case has been decided by a lower state or federal court, a litigant has the right to file a petition with the Supreme Court seeking a "writ of *certiorari*," the technical term for the writ the Supreme Court issues when it agrees to hear and decide an appeal.

Typically, the Court will consider something in the neighborhood of seven thousand such petitions a year. In the selection process, the justices look for cases of constitutional significance and other matters of national importance. After an initial screening process that eliminates most of the petitions, the justices meet to consider the remaining petitions on Wednesdays and Fridays in a secure conference room, in which no outsiders are allowed. The justices study the petitions well in advance of the conference, and after the chief justice opens the discussion by summarizing each case, each justice then speaks, in order of seniority. The most junior justice has the task of guarding the door: if reference materials or anything else is needed, the junior justice notifies an attendant stationed outside of the conference room, and then receives whatever was requested outside the door. No one enters the room.

It takes a vote of four justices to "grant cert," as it is colloquially called. If "cert" is not granted, the decision of the lower court remains undisturbed. From the thousands of petitions for *certiorari* it receives each year, in the 1980s the Court accepted approximately 150 cases per year on which it rendered written decisions. That number dropped to about 80 cases per year under Chief Justice Rehnquist. Recently appointed Chief Justice Roberts has indicated a desire to increase that number.

Each term begins on the first Monday in October. Well before each Court session, the lawyers representing the parties submit detailed briefs which the justices carefully study. During Court sessions, which are open to the public, the lawyers present oral arguments to the justices. Frequently, individual justices will interrupt and ask the lawyers difficult and pointed questions, sometimes for the purpose of honestly exploring the merits of an issue, sometimes for the purpose of reinforcing a favored position or tearing down a disfavored position in the hope of building support among the other justices.

After oral arguments, a conference is scheduled at which the justices discuss and vote on how they believe a case should be decided, at least at that point. If the chief justice is in the majority, he assigns either himself or another justice to write the majority opinion; if not, the senior justice who is in the majority makes that assignment. Other justices may write their own concurring or dissenting opinions. The opinions are then circulated among the justices in the effort to build as much consensus as possible. Debates continue, and opinions are revised, as the justices continue to exchange views among themselves.

Ultimately, each justice decides whether he or she will subscribe to the majority opinion. A justice who votes with the majority may also write a concurring opinion, explaining his or her own views. Justices who do not subscribe to the majority view may write dissenting opinions to explain the bases for their position. Most cases are decided clearly and decisively, but approximately 20 percent of the cases carry only a 5-4 majority, and some cases are so difficult and contentious that they generate numerous opinions, none of which garner the support of a majority.

What If the Supreme Court Issued an Order . . . and No One Listened?

It is frequently said that the Supreme Court has no army—a pithy way to make the point that the Supreme Court has no way to independently enforce its rulings. Consequently, the Court depends on the will of the other branches of government, usually the president, to carry out its decisions, as when troops were called in to enforce school desegregation after *Brown v. Board of Education.*

We take it for granted that what the Supreme Court says, goes. Still, there are nightmare scenarios that are difficult to contemplate. As many of the cases in the following chapters demonstrate, sometimes the Supreme Court has to take on the president head-on, and sometime a true reading of the Constitution requires the Court to take an exrremely unpopular position. If a president openly defied a Supreme Court order, what then? If the president were backed by the polls, would Congress have the political will to pursue impeachment in order to protect the Constitution? How would that battle play out?

These are the kinds of upheavals that plague countries without engrained constitutional traditions, where might makes right. At least for now, our tradition and culture make these scenarios unlikely; respect for the highest court's interpretation of the Constitution is, after all, at the root of what defines "a government of laws, not men."

But whether this remains the case will depend on whether the justices are viewed, beyond rational doubt, as serving only the Constitution, and not their own political agendas or social or religious philosophies. If the good faith of those who make up the Supreme Court ever comes into serious question, the moral authority of the Court—which is, really, the only authority the Court ultimately has—will evaporate, with disastrous results.

The following chapters explain some of the Supreme Court decisions that have had the greatest impact on our history and character, and that most affect the everyday lives of Americans. The intention is to enable the reader to appreciate the mammoth difficulty and consequence of the issues the Supreme Court has had to wrestle with, and to allow the reader to reach an informed judgment on whether the Supreme Court has earned its moral authority, or not.

Some of these decisions resonate from the past; others deal exclusively with twenty-first-century issues; all of them help define who we are and where we are going. They illuminate the tensions between individual liberty and the interests of society, the challenge of balancing majority rule with minority rights, the difficulties of applying old laws to new technologies and changing cultures, and the need to address crises in the short term while preserving fundamental rights in the long term. Like it or not, each of us, and our children who come after us, will be affected, even transformed, by what these decisions say.

Chapter 1
How the Supreme Court Became Supreme

"We are not final because we are infallible, but we are infallible only because we are final."
—Justice Robert H. Jackson

The Supreme Court was not always so supreme. It took the Supreme Court's own decision to create this prerogative—in effect, the Supreme Court created its own preeminence.

This seminal decision was rendered in the 1803 case of *Marbury v. Madison*, which gave the Supreme Court the right of "judicial review"—the power, mentioned previously, to determine what is and is not constitutional, and the coordinate right to void governmental actions and laws if they violate the Constitution. This power to ensure compliance with the Constitution not only defined the landscape of our own democracy, it served as a model for constitutional democracies throughout the world.

As would ultimately be seen, however, the power to decide takes with it the power to decide wrongly. And the impact of a wrong decision by the Supreme Court can change the face of society, reverberating for decades, even centuries.

1. MARBURY v. MADISON
Chief Justice Marshall 1803

Marbury v. Madison arose from the uncertainties that characterized the first years after the Constitution was ratified—no one could be sure of exactly what the Constitution would come to mean in practice, and the branches of government openly jockeyed for position. As for the Supreme Court, the framers had not specifically delineated how much influence it should have, and this issue provoked much debate and disagreement. Many felt that the most the Supreme Court could do was interpret laws, not overrule them. Indeed, in the early days of our country, the Supreme Court did not even have its own building (Congress graciously allowed it to conduct business in a committee room in the Capitol), and its role as an equal, let alone preeminent branch of government was anything but plain.

The seeds of change, however, were planted in 1800, when Republican Thomas Jefferson defeated incumbent Federalist John Adams in a bitterly contested election. Just before he left office, Adams attempted to entrench Federalist judges in the judiciary by appointing sixteen new circuit judges and forty-two new justices of the peace. However, due to a last-minute administrative mix-up as Adams left and Jefferson arrived, one of the appointees, Marbury, did not receive his written commission appointing him as a justice of the peace, even though it had been signed by then-president Adams and confirmed by the Senate.

Jefferson and the Republicans bore much hostility toward the Federalists, and Jefferson, flexing his political muscles and testing the boundaries of presidential power, refused to issue the commission to Marbury. In effect, Jefferson declared that he had the power to do what he pleased, and he dared Marbury to do something about it.

David Versus Goliath: Marbury Strikes Back

Marbury was incensed, and he turned to the courts for help. He sued the iconic James Madison, Jefferson's secretary of state (the government official in technical possession of the commission), seeking an order requiring that the commission be delivered to him. Jefferson was not pleased.

Marbury filed his lawsuit against Madison directly in the Supreme Court. Normally, a lawsuit would have to wend its way through the lower courts before the Supreme Court would even think about considering it, but Congress had passed a statute, the Judiciary Act of 1789, that allowed suits like the one brought by Marbury to bypass the lower courts and proceed in this rather unusual way.

Chief Justice Marshall felt that Marbury had been wronged by Jefferson, but he also felt that the Judiciary Act of 1789 violated the Constitution. Marshall's view was that the Constitution did not permit lawsuits like Marbury's to be filed in the Supreme Court, and he believed that Congress had overstepped its authority by enacting a statute that contradicted the Constitution's plain language.

Marshall's Masterstroke

Marbury's lawsuit presented on a silver platter the issue that Chief Justice Marshall longed to decide: whether the judiciary had the power to declare unconstitutional and therefore invalidate a law, in this case the Judiciary Act of 1789, that was passed by a duly elected legislature and signed by a duly elected president, each of which comprise an equal branch of government. How could the three branches of government be equal if, in fact, one could effectively negate the actions of the other? Or, as Marshall put it through superlative understatement, "The question, whether an act, repugnant to the constitution, can become the law of the land, is a question deeply interesting to the United States."

At the same time, Marshall realized that he was not merely deciding an important legal issue—he was defining the shape of the American system of government for succeeding generations. He knew that if he found in favor of Marbury and ordered Jefferson to issue the writ, Jefferson would likely ignore the order. He also knew that if he denied Marbury's claim, it would appear that the Court had kowtowed to the President. Either way, Marshall knew that depending on what he did, the Court could be forever relegated to second-class status. And, knowing his legacy rested in the balance, Marshall was not about to allow that to happen.

Marshall, as adept at politics as he was at law, crafted a solution that, to this day, is recognized as a consummate judicial tour de force.

Initially, Marshall declared that Marbury should have received his commission, chastising Jefferson, and avoiding the appearance of judicial subservience.

Marshall then ruled unconstitutional the act of Congress, the Judiciary Act of 1789, that gave the Supreme Court the power to hear Marbury's case and reverse what Jefferson had done. Bad news for Marbury, but in so doing Marshall dodged a confrontation with Jefferson, and simultaneously gave himself the opportunity to establish, once and for all, the right of the Supreme Court to void any law that the

Supreme Court deemed, in its sole judgment, to violate the Constitution. Marshall capitalized on that opportunity, using logic and language that has resonated throughout our history.

Marshall wrote that the American people had a right to "establish, for their future government, such principles as, in their opinion, shall most conduce to their own happiness," and had done so in the form of a written Constitution. The Constitution represents the "original and supreme will" of the people and "is the basis on which the whole American fabric has been erected." From this, Marshall's ultimate conclusion, on which so much of America as it exists today is founded, logically followed:

> Certainly, all those who have framed written constitutions contemplate them as forming the fundamental and paramount law of the nations, and, consequently, the theory of every such government must be, that an act of the legislature, repugnant to the constitution, is void.

The Legacy of *Marbury v. Madison*

Consider where we might be had Chief Justice Marshall not taken this judicial leap of faith. Without *Marbury v. Madison* and the principles it entrenched, Congress, or a state legislature, or a local borough council would only be restrained by the fear of losing the next election. So long as the majority of voters remained either in favor of or apathetic about what government did, government officials could pass laws designed to eliminate free speech among their critics, arbitrarily restrict the use of private property, favor their race or religion over others, gerrymander election districts to effectively fix elections, and so on. In essence, they could do whatever they wanted for so long as they could successfully manipulate the political process and stay in office.

But after *Marbury v. Madison* the rulebook changed, and the players had to change along with it: now, government officials know that at any time, a single citizen armed with a creative lawyer can invoke the power of the judiciary to measure their laws and decisions against constitutional standards. Each citizen, through this right to invoke the overriding authority of the Constitution, can play a direct role in controlling government, instead of government controlling each citizen. *Marbury v. Madison* gave us the opportunity to remain the government of laws, not men, that is a prime hallmark of our greatness as a nation.

To this day, virtually all constitutional law courses begin with *Marbury v. Madison,* and constitutional democracies throughout the world revere the decision as the wellspring of the checks and balances that make a true and lasting democracy feasible.

2. DRED SCOTT v. SANFORD
Did the Supreme Court Trigger the Civil War?
1857

The infamous *Dred Scott v. Sanford* decision was the first case since *Marbury v. Madison*, decided more than fifty years earlier, in which the Supreme Court used the power of judicial review to declare an act of Congress unconstitutional. It had all the elements of a Hollywood thriller—human pathos, a burning national crisis, backroom deals, moral activists facing off against big business, ethical weakness at the highest levels of government, the rise of an unknown crusader into the pantheon of history. Everything, that is, except a happy ending. The *Dred Scott* case reinforced the role of the Supreme Court as the institution to which American society turns for the final and binding decisions on its most incendiary issues. It also serves as the exemplar of how much damage can be done when the power of judicial review goes awry.

At its core, in the *Dred Scott* decision the Supreme Court ruled that slaves and free blacks were not citizens worthy of constitutional protection, and could lawfully be claimed as property, even in states that had outlawed slavery. The decision placed a stamp of approval on slavery, put a match to an already smoldering blood feud between North and South, and accelerated a chain of events that ultimately elected Lincoln and overwhelmed whatever opportunity there had been to avoid civil war.

This "self-inflicted wound" (as one future justice described the case) seriously diminished the prestige and power of the Court for at least a generation.

Dred Scott's Suit for Freedom

After the ratification of the Constitution (which purposefully failed to confront the legalities of slavery), the bitter fight between pro-slavery and anti-slavery forces intensified. This led, in 1820, to the Missouri Compromise—as part of the admission of Maine and Missouri as states, Congress provided that (with the exception of Missouri itself) slavery would be prohibited in the territories north of the line that formed Missouri's southern border.

Dred Scott was a Virginia slave who had been sold to an army physician, Dr. Emerson, who took him north of the Missouri Compromise line (where slavery was unlawful), and then back to Missouri (where slavery was lawful). In prior cases, numerous courts had ruled and it was generally accepted that once a slave set foot on free soil, he was emancipated. In 1850, Scott, who had saved some money, tried to buy his freedom from Dr. Emerson's widow, who now owned Scott. Dr. Emerson's widow refused, and Scott brought suit in Missouri state court claiming that, having lived in the free territory, he was now a free man.

A jury found in Scott's favor, but the Missouri Supreme Court reversed, ruling that it was "a humiliating spectacle to see a court of a state confiscate the property of her own citizens by the command of a foreign law." In other words, Dred Scott was *property*, and a contrary law enacted by a Congress situated far away, in Washington, DC, was a "foreign law" that need not be followed.

Dred Scott's attorney responded by dropping his claims in state court, and filing a lawsuit in federal court. Scott's position was this: citizens can sue in federal court; Scott was a citizen by virtue of his journey to a free territory; and the Missouri Compromise, a federal law, should be enforced for his benefit.

Scott lost, and the Supreme Court accepted the appeal.

Scott's case crystallized the most combustible issues of the time. Is a freed black a "citizen" who is entitled to protection under the Constitution, or merely property to be bought and sold? Does the federal government have the constitutional power to tell the states what to do about slavery?

As the Supreme Court mulled over the issues, the country became embroiled in a hurricane of pro-slavery versus anti-slavery debate. As emotions rose, Stephen A. Douglas, a well-known Illinois senator and orator, introduced a bill in Congress that sought to invalidate the Missouri Compromise in Kansas and Nebraska so that those states could decide the slavery issue for themselves, free from federal interference. This further outraged the North, and a new party was formed, the Republican Party, which passionately opposed the extension of slavery into the territories. Angry and concerned citizens in both the North and South gathered and argued on street corners and in town halls.

The Decision and Its Aftermath: North v. South

Chief Justice Taney announced the Supreme Court's decision on March 6, 1857. Joined by six other justices, he wrote that blacks had been regarded as holding an inferior status when the Constitution was adopted, and were therefore not "citizens" entitled to sue in federal court. That ruling effectively put Dred Scott out of court, and there was no reason for the decision to go further. But Chief Justice Taney did not stop there.

Invoking the Court's judicial review powers, Chief Justice Taney went on to rule that Congress had exceeded its constitutional authority when it enacted the Missouri Compromise. As a result, Dred Scott could no longer argue that because he had been taken to a free territory he was therefore emancipated—the Missouri Compromise was invalid and without legal effect, and consequently the territory north of the Missouri Compromise line was no longer free. Moreover, said Chief Justice Taney, it would be unconstitutional to deem a slave a free man merely because the slave had been taken into free territory, since that would deprive the slave owner of his rightful property, the slave, without just compensation: the government could not take a man's farm or livestock without paying him, and neither could it take a man's slaves.

The upshot was that slaves were to remain slaves, and the federal government had been stripped of the authority to do much about it.

Even formerly apathetic Northerners took the decision as a virtual call to arms, swelling the ranks of the militant abolitionists. Horace Greeley, a famed journalist and politician, owned the most influential newspaper of the time, the *New York Tribune*, in which he wrote that the Dred Scott decision "is entitled to just so much moral weight as would be the judgment of a majority of those congregated in any Washington bar-room." At the same time, the South was empowered, and Southern politicians and newspapers trumpeted the decision as a validation of states' rights, in particular the right of any established or new state to decide whether slavery would be legal within its borders, no matter what the federal government said.

Cynics speculated that some of the Supreme Court justices had been influenced by politics. President Buchanan (who had won the election, but was awaiting his inauguration) made no secret of the fact that he opposed the Missouri Compromise and wanted it overturned. In recent years, historians have uncovered evidence of patently unethical communications in which Buchanan lobbied at least two of the justices to sign on to Taney's opinion.

Lincoln Enters the Controversy

A year after the *Dred Scott* decision was announced, Lincoln, then an unknown on the national stage, challenged Douglas, then a leading candidate for the Democratic presidential nomination, for Douglas's Illinois senate seat. Lincoln initiated his campaign with one of his most famous speeches. He stressed the injustice in the fact that, according to the *Dred Scott* decision, a slave could live in a free state and, yet, still be a slave. Said Lincoln, "A house divided against itself cannot stand. I believe this government cannot endure, permanently half slave and half free." In the months that followed, the candidates engaged in the famous Lincoln-Douglas debates, in which Lincoln repeatedly railed at the *Dred Scott* decision and all those who agreed that blacks were not entitled to protection under the precepts of the Declaration of Independence and the Constitution.

Douglas sought a middle ground, and in the process alienated both Northern and Southern voters. In the 1860 presidential campaign, Douglas got the Democratic nomination, but Southerners bolted from the party and nominated their own pro-slavery ticket. The Whigs also nominated their own ticket, and riding the crest of the notoriety he obtained after *Dred Scott*, the Republican Party nominated Lincoln. This four-party election fractionalized the electorate—Lincoln received a minority of the popular vote, but won the electoral vote and, ironically, was sworn in as president by Chief Justice Taney himself, in 1861.

Lincoln immediately faced Northerners who believed the *Dred Scott* decision would lead to future Supreme Court cases in which Northern states would be forbidden from banning slavery within their borders (and Lincoln himself fanned those flames in the Lincoln-Douglas debates). At the same time, he was confronted by Southerners who celebrated the prospect of slave auctions on the Boston Commons.

The rest, as the saying goes, is history.

Ultimately, the Fourteenth Amendment, adopted in 1868, provided that slaves were fully entitled to citizenship and constitutional protections, effectively overruling the *Dred Scott* decision and launching it into ignominy. That did little good in reality, however, as the so-called Black Codes of the Southern states imposed second-class status, and much worse, on Southern blacks until the federal government enacted and began to enforce, sometimes through military actions, meaningful civil rights legislation in the 1960s.

As for Dred Scott himself, in 1857, Dr. Emerson's widow remarried. Her new husband opposed slavery, and she returned Scott to his former owners, the Blow family, who gave Scott and his family their freedom. The next year, Dred Scott died of tuberculosis. His gravesite in St. Louis County now bears the following marker:

> DRED SCOTT BORN ABOUT 1799 DIED SEPT. 17,
> 1858. DRED SCOTT SUBJECT OF THE DECISION
> OF THE SUPREME COURT OF THE UNITED STATES
> IN 1857 WHICH DENIED CITIZENSHIP TO THE
> NEGRO, VOIDED THE MISSOURI COMPROMISE
> ACT, BECAME ONE OF THE EVENTS THAT
> RESULTED IN THE CIVIL WAR.

Chapter 2
One Nation Under God? Matters of Church and State

"A union of government and religion tends to destroy government and degrade religion."
—Justice Hugo L. Black

The phrase "separation of church and state" is engrained in the American vernacular but, contrary to the common mythology, the phrase does not appear in the Constitution. Jefferson lobbied for, as he put it, "a wall of separation between church and state," but other Founding Fathers sought no more than a constitutional provision forbidding the government from enshrining a national religion. They wanted religious freedom, and feared the religious persecution that would result if government were permitted to endorse one religion over another.

When all was said and done, the framers of the Constitution inserted into the First Amendment a provision known as the "Establishment Clause," which as now interpreted effectively provides that government "shall make no law respecting an establishment of religion."

The disagreement over what those words shall mean has spurred an ongoing constitutional holy war in which the hostilities continue, while the battlegrounds change.

3. ENGEL v. VITALE
The School Prayer Case: Religion in the Public Schools 1962

Legal scholars have debated the meaning of the Establishment Clause for decades. The words themselves do not reflect the adoption of Jefferson's point of view: there is no mandate that *all* religion be removed from the public arena. Still, at what point does the government's acceptance of or involvement in religion become "an establishment of religion"?

After a history of confusing and contradictory decisions, the Supreme Court began to clarify the practical meaning and impact of the Establishment Clause in the school prayer cases that captured the attention of the nation in the early 1960s.

Does School Prayer "Establish" Religion?

In many schools throughout the country, students were routinely required to begin the day with the recitation of a prayer. In New York, the state Board of Regents composed what they believed was a nondenominational prayer: "Almighty God, we acknowledge our dependence upon Thee, and we beg Thy blessing upon us, our parents, our teachers and our Country." The Regents suggested, but did not mandate, that the prayer be recited by all students at the commencement of each school day.

Claiming that the Regents' actions violated the Establishment Clause, a group of parents filed a lawsuit, *Engel v. Vitale*, which worked its way through the court system, and eventually was heard by the Supreme Court.

Facing extreme pressure on both sides of the issue, a

clear majority of the Supreme Court agreed that the Regents had overstepped their constitutional boundaries. Justice Black, writing for the majority, put the issue into its historical context, recalling "that this very practice of establishing governmentally composed prayers for religious services was one of the reasons which caused many of our early colonists to leave England and seek religious freedom in America." Justice Black reasoned that a prayer is by its very nature religious, and that "we think that the constitutional prohibition against laws respecting an establishment of religion must at least mean that in this country it is no part of the business of government to compose official prayers for any group of the American people to recite as a part of a religious program carried on by government."

New York (and the many other states that supported its position) argued that the prayer could not constitute the establishment of religion because it was voluntary, and did not reference any particular faith. Justice Black was unpersuaded. The prayer, he reasoned, promotes religion, and that is enough, even if it is not coercive. And the fact that the prayer referred to no particular religion is inconsequential, since it still promotes a family of religions—those that believe in "Almighty God."

The Court's ultimate ruling was plainly stated: "We think that by using its public school system to encourage recitation of the Regents' prayer, the State of New York has adopted a practice wholly inconsistent with the Establishment Clause."

The rationale of *Engel v. Vitale*, handed down in 1962, was expanded and clarified the next year in the case of *Abington Township School District v. Schempp*, which declared the practice of school-sponsored Bible reading and the recitation of the Lord's Prayer to be similarly unconstitutional. The *Schempp* case is doubly significant. In it, the Supreme Court also laid down what is known as the "secular purpose" and "primary effect" tests for Establishment Clause cases: if either the purpose or the effect of a law or government action is to advance or inhibit religion, the Establishment Clause is implicated. Using these criteria, as well as similar criteria that evolved in subsequent Establishment Clause cases, the Supreme Court has ruled unconstitutional all manner of school-sponsored or school-endorsed prayers at graduation ceremonies and other school events.

The "Religion-Free Zone" Myth

The *Engel* and *Schempp* cases were the subject of much protest, and in the process their true meaning has become substantially distorted.

Neither case, as is so often stated, takes God out of the schools, or mandates that schools be "religion-free zones." *Engel* and *Schempp* in no way restrict the teaching of religion as a subject of academic study, and they do not prohibit individual students from saying a prayer, distributing religious literature, talking to students about their religious beliefs, forming Bible study groups, or wearing religious clothing, subject to the same rules of orderly conduct and school administration as other, nonreligious behavior. The Supreme Court placed its focus on the role of government in *promoting* religion, not the role of students in *practicing* religion.

Even so, disagreements over the meaning of the Establishment Clause continue to abound. Many citizens (including several Supreme Court justices) stress that the framers of the Constitution were men who held not only an abiding belief in God, but also a belief that the nation itself owed its existence and future to God. Therefore, they argue, while the framers did indeed fear the establishment of a "state religion," they could not have intended to invalidate prayers and ceremonies that do no more than pay respect to God.

Engel and *Schempp* have been settled law for over forty years, and barring a dramatic shift in the makeup of the Court it is unlikely they will be overturned. On the school front, the Establishment Clause battleground has shifted from school ceremonies to school curriculum. The next battery of Supreme Court decisions in this area will likely define the difference between that which constitutes the teaching of science, ethics, or philosophy and that which constitutes the promotion and sponsorship of religion.

4. EPPERSON v. ARKANSAS

The Scopes "Monkey Trial" Revisited: The Teaching of Evolution, Creationism, and Intelligent Design in Public Schools 1968

In the 1920s, fundamentalist religious groups lobbied public schools to prohibit the teaching of evolution, linking it with atheism. William Jennings Bryan, former secretary of state, three-time presidential candidate, famous orator and a staunch fundamentalist, personally championed this movement, labeling the teaching of evolution irrational and immoral. (As Bryan was fond of saying during his many orations, "It is better to trust in the Rock of Ages than to know the ages of rock.") Largely as a result of his efforts, in 1925, Tennessee passed a law, known as the Butler Act, which forbade the teaching in public schools of "any theory that denies the story of the Divine Creation of man as taught in the Bible, and to teach instead that man has descended from a lower order of animals."

The Scopes "Monkey Trial"

The ACLU immediately offered to defend anyone convicted under the Butler Act. Sensing an opportunity to bring publicity and commerce to their town, within a few months a group of businessmen in Dayton, Tennessee, convinced a local biology teacher, John Scopes, to admit that he taught evolution, and to invite prosecution as a test case. The prosecutors obliged.

Bryan immediately accepted an invitation to assist the prosecution. In response, Clarence Darrow, a staunch agnostic and one of the most famous lawyers and social crusaders of his day, volunteered to help the defense. The famous Scopes "Monkey Trial" was on.

The trial was covered by more than a hundred newspaper reporters from all parts of the country, as well as reporters from Europe. Twenty-two telegraphers sent out 165,000 words a day, and a Chicago radio station broadcast the trial nationally—the first live radio coverage of a criminal trial. Two movie cameramen had their film flown out daily from a specially prepared airstrip.

The defense originally challenged the Butler Act on Establishment Clause grounds, but Darrow took control, launched a frontal assault on Bryan himself, and called Bryan as a witness in the effort to get Bryan to admit that whatever moral and religious teachings the Bible might provide, it was not "science" and could not be taken literally. Darrow's cross examination of Bryan became the stuff of legend. Darrow took Bryan through the story of Jonah, accounts of the earth standing still, the story of creation as set forth in Genesis, whether Eve was actually created from Adam's rib, and so on. The exchanges between the two were blistering. Bryan accused Darrow of having no purpose other than "to cast ridicule on everybody who believes in the Bible." Darrow responded, "We have the purpose of preventing bigots and ignoramuses from controlling the education of the United States." (The play and movie, *Inherit the Wind*, dramatizes the trial, and the Darrow-Bryan confrontation in particular, but does so with much poetic license.)

Darrow knew that he could not possibly obtain an acquittal in the Dayton trial court—it was never contested that Scopes violated the Butler Act. He also knew that a challenge to the constitutionality of the Butler Act would be better pursued before an appeals court. Rather than trying to win the case in Dayton, Darrow's intent was to ridicule Bryan's position and turn public opinion against statutes like the Butler Act, and by many accounts he plainly succeeded. H. L. Mencken, a famous journalist who actually helped fund the defense, wrote that Bryan was a "buffoon" and that his speeches were "theologic bilge," while characterizing the defense as "eloquent" and "magnificent." *Life* magazine awarded Bryan its "Brass Medal of the Fourth Class," writing that he had "successfully demonstrated by the alchemy of ignorance hot air may be transmuted into gold, and that the Bible is infallibly inspired except where it differs with him on the question of wine, women, and wealth."

Outfoxing Bryan, at the close of the trial Darrow literally told the judge to find Scopes guilty, and Darrow gave no final summation. Under Tennessee procedures, if Darrow gave no final summation, Bryan would be barred from making a final summation as well. Darrow knew that Bryan had been hungering to deliver a speech that Bryan later called "the mountain peak of my life's effort," a fire-and-brimstone, anti-evolution, fundamentalist oration for the assembled journalists and radio audience, and Darrow's tactic ended the trial before Bryan had his opportunity.

After nine minutes of deliberation, the jury found Scopes guilty, and the judge ordered him to pay a $100 fine (which Bryan offered to pay on Scopes's behalf). The defense appealed to the Tennessee Supreme Court. Among other arguments, the defense contended that the Butler Act violated the Establishment Clause, and was therefore unconstitutional. The Tennessee Supreme Court refused to so rule—but found an "out" and reversed the conviction anyway, ruling that under Tennessee law, the jury, not the judge, was to have decided the amount of the fine.

Having had enough, the prosecution never sought a retrial. The "Monkey Trial" remained part of American history and legend, but had no significant impact on American law for more than forty years. In the meantime, the anti-evolutionists vigorously continued their efforts, and laws similar to the Butler Act were enacted in Mississippi and Arkansas. The ACLU was unable to find another teacher willing to go through what Scopes had endured, and it was not until the 1960s, spurred by the Supreme Court's Establishment Clause decisions in the school prayer cases, that the issue was again pursued, culminating in the Supreme Court's 1968 decision in *Epperson v. Arkansas*.

The Scopes "Monkey Trial" Redux

Arkansas' anti-evolution statute, passed in 1928, was in practical effect identical to the Butler Act, making it a crime "to teach the theory or doctrine that mankind ascended or descended from a lower order of animals" or "to adopt or use in any such institution a textbook" that holds this view. No one had ever been prosecuted under the law, but the Arkansas Education Association sought to challenge it on Establishment Clause grounds and, ultimately, it convinced a high school teacher, Susan Epperson, to do so. The Arkansas Education Association brought a lawsuit in her name, seeking to have the law invalidated.

After a one-day trial, an Arkansas trial court judge ruled that the Arkansas law was unconstitutional, but the Arkansas attorney general appealed, and the Arkansas Supreme Court then reinstated the law as "a valid exercise of the state's power to specify the curriculum in its public schools." The Supreme Court accepted the appeal in order to finally settle the issue the Scopes "Monkey Trial" had raised but not resolved: whether states could ban the teaching of evolution in public schools, or whether such a ban was unconstitutional.

The result: a unanimous Supreme Court ruled that a ban on the teaching of evolution violates the Establishment Clause.

Justice Fortas, writing for the majority, explained that the Establishment Clause mandates that government maintain a position of neutrality in religious matters. "Government in our democracy, state and national, must be neutral in matters of religious theory, doctrine, and practice. It may not be hostile to any religion or to the advocacy of no-religion; and it may not aid, foster, or promote one religion or religious theory against another." Contrary to this tenet of law, the Court found that the sole reason for the Arkansas law was that a particular religious group considered the theory of evolution to be in conflict with the Bible's account of creation, a view that group favored. As a result, the Court ruled that "Arkansas' law cannot be defended as an act of religious neutrality."

The Evolution of the Creationists

Creationists responded with a switch in tactics. Rather than outlawing the teaching of evolution altogether, they successfully passed "equal time" or "balanced treatment" statutes that mandated that both evolution and "creation science" be taught. The rationale for these laws, went the argument, was that the teaching of various scientific theories would advance the cause of science instruction generally, which was a secular, nonreligious purpose beyond the reach of the Establishment Clause.

These efforts eventually found their way to the Supreme

Court, in the 1987 decision in *Edwards v. Aguillar*, which directly confronted the issue of whether "creation science" was really science, or religion in scientific clothing. Seventy-two Nobel Prize–winning scientists, seventeen state academies of science, and seven other scientific organizations urged that "creation science" was, in fact, religion.

By a 7-2 majority, the Supreme Court agreed. The Court found that "the term 'creation science' . . . embodies the religious belief that a supernatural creator was responsible for the creation of humankind." This, said the Court, documented that "creation science" had as its primary purpose the advancement of a particular religious viewpoint—that is, the belief in a supreme being—and was therefore at odds with the Establishment Clause.

The *Edwards* decision, however, was equally unsuccessful in ending these confrontations. After *Edwards*, opponents of the teaching of evolution promoted the concept of "intelligent design" as a curriculum that could be taught in the public schools without offending the Establishment Clause. Intelligent design points to the gaps in the theory of evolution, contends that nature exhibits a "purposeful arrangement of parts," and posits that an "intelligent designer" must therefore have been involved in creation generally and mankind in particular—but does not go so far as to state directly that the "intelligent designer" must be God.

The constitutionality of teaching "intelligent design" is being actively litigated in the lower courts. Almost inevitably, the proponents and opponents of intelligent design will eventually find their way to the Supreme Court, where yet another chapter of the book that began with the Scopes "Monkey Trial" will be written.

5. VAN ORDEN v. PERRY

6. MCCREARY COUNTY, KENTUCKY v. ACLU OF KENTUCKY

The Ten Commandments Cases: Religion in the Public Square 2005

The school prayer and creationism cases provided substantial clarity to the dispute over religion in the public schools. But what about religion in the public square?

In two Supreme Court cases decided in 2005, the Supreme Court determined whether state-sponsored displays of the Ten Commandments violate the Establishment Clause. In these cases, *Van Orden v. Perry* and *McCreary County, Kentucky v. ACLU of Kentucky,* the Supreme Court has revealed much about where, and how, it will draw the boundaries between church and state in the years to come.

Approximately forty years ago, a patriotic organization presented Texas with a six-foot monolith inscribed with the Ten Commandments. Texas chose to display the monument on state land at state expense, between the Texas State Capitol and the Texas Supreme Court, among approximately twenty other monuments of varying types and themes. More recently, two Kentucky counties posted large, highly visible copies of the Ten Commandments in their courthouses.

Both displays were challenged in court—the *Van Orden* case arose out of the Texas display, and the *McCreary* case arose out of the Kentucky display. The issue in both cases was whether displaying the Ten Commandments on public property brought church and state too close together, in violation of the Establishment Clause. The Supreme Court, seeking an opportunity to clarify how separate church and state must be, agreed to hear the appeals of these cases.

By a 5-4 margin, the Court ruled that *some* intermixture between church and state is permissible, and that the Texas display did *not* violate the Establishment Clause. However, the Court also ruled that too much intermixture is impermissible, and that the Kentucky display *did* violate the Establishment Clause. Where is the line, and how does one find it?

Similar to the analysis in the *Schempp* school prayer case discussed previously, and relying on similar cases decided in other contexts, the Supreme Court looked for the *purpose*, the *effect*, and the *context* of the religious displays.

The Texas Ten Commandments monument was part of a larger display that highlighted the role of both religious and secular influences in law, government, and history. Admittedly, the Ten Commandments is a religious icon, but to the majority of the justices, the purpose and effect of the Texas Ten Commandments display was not primarily religious, in the sense of extolling the Ten Commandments for its spiritual content, but rather it focused on the historical and cultural role of the Ten Commandments in a larger, nonreligious context. The 5-4 majority allowed the Texas monument to stand for these reasons.

But the same could not be said about the Kentucky display. The Ten Commandments display was put there by itself, within no larger historic or cultural context, and for no apparent purpose other than to endorse the Ten Commandments for its own sake. Because there was no independent, secular reason to justify the display of a religious symbol, the 5-4 majority required that the Kentucky display be removed.

How Much Religion Is Too Much Religion?

What do the *McCreary* and *Van Orden* decisions bode for the future of church-state relationships?

The fact that the Supreme Court will not mandate anything approaching a total "separation of church and state" was a foregone conclusion; after all, as has been the tradition for many years, every Supreme Court session begins with a Supreme Court official intoning, "God save the United States and this Honorable Court," and it is not likely that the "In God We Trust" inscription will be removed from the money supply anytime soon.

But *McCreary* and *Van Orden* do confirm the ground rules by which future church-state issues will be analyzed and decided. Are government grants that support "faith-based" organizations constitutional? *McCreary* and *Van Orden* seem to say that if the purpose and effect of the money, and the context in which the money is given, is religion-neutral and pertains primarily to a secular purpose, like feeding the hungry, the fact that a religious group gets an incidental benefit does not matter. What about challenges to the phrase "under God" in the Pledge of Allegiance? Are the purpose, effect, and context of the Pledge the promotion of a belief in God, or is the Pledge primarily geared toward an acknowledgment of the role a belief in God has played in the country's history and culture since the Constitution was drafted. What about the teaching of "intelligent design" as part of the science curriculum in public schools? Is its purpose and effect to promote a belief in God, or does it represent a good faith attempt to promote scientific inquiry within an educational context?

To be sure, there will be lots of "wiggle room" within the parameters defined by the *McCreary* and *Van Orden* decisions, but a tone has been set: government support of religion primarily for the sake of religion itself will be prohibited, but many other forms of government entanglement with religion will be permitted.

———◆◆◆———

Chapter 3
Innocent Until Proven Guilty:
The Rights of the Accused

*"Better that ten guilty persons escape
than that one innocent suffer."*
—William Blackstone,
eighteenth-century English jurist

Our Founding Fathers were mindful of the penchant of
monarchs to charge persons with false crimes as a means of
political oppression and social control. Consequently, they
built copious protections for those accused of criminal
offenses into the foundations of the Constitution. It was
acknowledged that giving all benefits of the doubt to the
accused would result in some guilty persons being set free
and, yet, they freely accepted this necessary evil as a price
of freedom.

The story is told of a Chinese law professor who was
advised of our belief that it was better that a thousand
guilty men go free than one innocent man be executed.
The Chinese professor thought for a bit, and asked, "Better
for whom?"

The Founding Fathers' answer to that question was this:
better for all, because as history has proven, if *anyone* can
be unlawfully jailed, *everyone* can be unlawfully jailed.

7. GIDEON v. WAINWRIGHT

The Right to Be Represented by Counsel When Charged With a Crime 1963

The Sixth Amendment to the Constitution provides that in criminal prosecutions, the accused has the right "to have the Assistance of Counsel for his defence." Based on this constitutional mandate, federal courts have for many years appointed lawyers for criminal defendants who are without the means to hire a lawyer on their own. However, until the 1960s, the law was unclear as to whether the Sixth Amendment also applied to the states, where the vast majority of the criminal prosecutions took place. As a result, the Supreme Court left it to each state to decide for itself whether indigent defendants charged in state courts would be provided with lawyers—and this resulted in innumerable unrepresented people being convicted of crimes they claimed they did not commit.

In 1961, Clarence Gideon was accused of robbing a pool hall in Florida, and was charged with various crimes in a Florida state court. Gideon could not afford a lawyer, and at his trial he asked the judge to appoint a lawyer for him so that, as promised by the Sixth Amendment, he could have the assistance of counsel. The judge refused, in compliance with Florida law at the time, and Gideon was left to defend himself. Gideon maintained that he was innocent but, unschooled in the law, he did not do a good job at his trial. He was convicted and sentenced to five years in jail.

Gideon's Trumpet

From his jail cell, Gideon wrote out a petition to the Supreme Court of the United States. Gideon's position was simply this: an individual's ability to exercise his constitutional rights, in this case his Sixth Amendment right to have the assistance of counsel, should not depend on his wealth, or anything else. All Americans should have the same constitutional rights, in theory *and* in practice.

The Supreme Court agreed to hear Gideon's appeal. At the root of the case was this issue: could a defendant in a criminal case conceivably get a fair trial without the assistance of a lawyer?

In its decision, the Supreme Court detailed the extent to which our courts are subject to specialized procedures and rules, and the fact that the knowledge and skill required to assemble and conduct a defense take years of training and experience to acquire. As a result, the Court reasoned, "The right to be heard would be, in many cases, of little avail if it did not comprehend the right to be heard by counsel." Without counsel, the Court concluded, an innocent defendant "faces the danger of conviction because he does not know how to establish his innocence."

On these bases, the Supreme Court invalidated Gideon's conviction, ordered a retrial, and required that a lawyer be appointed to defend him. At his new trial, with the help of a lawyer, Gideon was acquitted of the crime.

Fifty years ago, it was routine for indigent persons to be charged with crimes and forced to defend themselves in state courts without the assistance of a lawyer; that scenario is now constitutionally unimaginable. Clarence Gideon changed the law, inspiring the book and movie *Gideon's Trumpet* (with Henry Fonda playing Gideon). As Robert F. Kennedy put it, "If an obscure Florida convict named Clarence Earl Gideon had not sat down in his prison cell . . .

to write a letter to the Supreme Court . . . the vast machinery of American law would have gone on functioning undisturbed. But Gideon did write that letter, the Court did look into his case . . . and the whole course of American legal history has been changed."

8. MIRANDA v. ARIZONA

"You Have the Right to Remain Silent . . .": The Privilege Against Self-Incrimination 1966

Consider this situation. A kidnapping and sexual assault occurs. The police arrest a suspect and take him to the police station, where he is identified by the victim. In accordance with standard operating procedures, the suspect is then taken into a private interrogation room. The suspect is not advised that he has the right to be represented by a lawyer before he is questioned. Two hours later, the suspect signs a confession. There is no evidence that the suspect was physically or mentally abused in any way. The confession includes a statement that the suspect has "full knowledge of my legal rights, understanding any statement I make may be used against me," and that he had knowingly waived those rights. The suspect is put on trial, the confession is read to the jury, and the suspect is convicted.

Anything wrong with that?

These are the basic facts in the famous *Miranda* case, decided in 1966, in which the Supreme Court, in a 5-4 decision, ruled that once Ernesto Miranda was taken into police custody and before any interrogation could begin, the police had the constitutional duty under the Fifth Amendment to advise him that he had the right to refuse to answer any questions and to be represented by a lawyer, and if Miranda chose to take advantage of those rights, the police could not interrogate him in any way. Because the police failed to advise Miranda of these rights—now known as *"Miranda rights"*—before they questioned him and obtained his confession, Miranda's conviction was thrown out, just as innumerable convictions since the *Miranda* decision have been thrown out for similar reasons.

Taking the Fifth

The Fifth Amendment to the Constitution commands that no person "shall be compelled in any criminal case to be a witness against himself." As fundamental as this right is, however, it has an image problem. The Fifth Amendment is popularly viewed as a "legal technicality"—a loophole guilty people can use in the effort to beat the system. In television and movies, street-savvy punks and sophisticated white-collar criminals smugly refuse to answer questions in the police station, while they mock the detectives' impotence. The evening news televises congressional hearings in which reputed organized crime figures and alleged corporate looters mechanically recite, "I assert my Fifth Amendment right against self-incrimination."

But the Fifth Amendment is anything but a legal technicality or a loophole.

It is easier and quicker for law enforcement authorities to solve a crime by coercing a confession than it is to solve a crime through tedious investigation, particularly where the evidence may be hard to come by. In the seventeenth century, this fact of life led to horrific injustices in England (and elsewhere), in which innocent people were jailed on the basis of confessions made only after physical abuse or threats of harm. In reaction (some say revolution) against these wrongs, the right against self-incrimination—that is, the right to make law enforcement prove its case without the testimony of the suspect—became entrenched as a bedrock principle of English law. The Founding Fathers brought this precept with them to the colonies. They knew the horrors of the old world too well, and resolved to build the right against self-incrimination into the framework of the Constitution.

Still, the issue the Supreme Court faced in *Miranda* was different. By the time the *Miranda* case arose, it was a given that the police could not coerce a suspect to confess, and then use that confession against him. And even Miranda's lawyers did not argue that anyone coerced a confession out of Miranda: he was put into an interrogation room, confronted by the police, and after a couple of hours of questioning he signed a statement.

Ignorance of the Law *Can* Be an Excuse

The Supreme Court ruled that this was not enough to protect Miranda's Fifth Amendment rights. It reviewed the many studies showing how subtle, psychological techniques can be used to intimidate unsophisticated suspects into signing an untrue confession. The Fifth Amendment, said the Court, prohibits much more than beatings with rubber hoses and the "third degree."

More important, the Supreme Court ruled that the Fifth Amendment is so crucial that law enforcement officials must make certain that a suspect is aware of the right to remain silent and the right to counsel, before any questioning can take place—and the rule applies not only when the police seek to directly question a suspect, but also when the try to elicit incriminating evidence through intimidation or manipulation techniques. If the suspect then intelligently and voluntarily waives his rights, so be it, but you cannot waive a right until you know that the right exists, and it is up to law enforcement to make certain that persons in their custody have this knowledge. Otherwise, said the Court, the potential for abuse is far greater than is tolerable in a civilized society.

After *Miranda* was decided, television viewers and moviegoers were routinely treated to chase scenes in which sprinting police officers tackle desperate criminals, at which time one of the officers triumphantly instructs an underling, "Read him his rights" ("You have the right to remain silent, anything you say can and will be used against you in a court of law . . .").

In this context, *Miranda* rights seem formulaic and silly, and it is easy to ignore their true significance. But the message of the case is of colossal importance: every individual accused of a crime has the right and the power to require that the government prove its accusations through real, substantive evidence, and every individual is provided with safeguards, like a lawyer and an unbiased court, to fend off the ability of those in power to get you if they want to.

As for Ernesto Miranda himself, his confession was thrown out. The police assembled the evidence, retried him, and Miranda was convicted.

Chapter 4
The Melting Pot: Race, Discrimination, and Diversity

"The one place where a man ought to get a square deal is in a courtroom, be he any color of the rainbow . . ."
—Atticus Finch,
in *To Kill a Mockingbird* by Harper Lee

It has often been observed that the history of America is in many ways the history of race relations. The Supreme Court has written much of that history, often with regrettable results. Ultimately, however, the Court turned prior law on its head, declared racial segregation unconstitutional, and literally changed America. The resulting anti-discrimination inertia not only led to expanded rights for minorities, it also launched anti-discrimination efforts in many other contexts, such as gender, age, religion, nationality, and sexual orientation, to name a few.

But here's the complication. Where is the line between prohibiting discrimination against individuals based on, for instance, their race or nationality, and *favoring* individuals based on their race or nationality? Isn't that discrimination, in reverse? And what about the right of people to be left alone? If they want to associate only with people of their own race, or gender, or sexual orientation, should the law be able to stop them?

9. BROWN v. BOARD OF EDUCATION

Separate Is Not Equal: The End of Legalized Segregation 1954

The aftermath of slavery plagued the twentieth century, as segregation remained a practical reality throughout much of the North, and was mandated by law throughout the South. Blacks attempted to challenge segregation in the courts, but in 1896, in the case of *Plessy v. Ferguson,* the Supreme Court openly endorsed the concept of "separate but equal." On the basis of that precedent, local courts, as well as the Supreme Court itself, repeatedly refused to rule that segregation in education (or anything else) was unconstitutional.

In the 1930s, the NAACP developed a legal strategy to challenge the "separate but equal" concept: in school after school, it successfully showed that the separate educational facilities being provided to blacks were not equal, and were vastly inferior. By the 1950s, however, the NAACP's legal team—led by Thurgood Marshall, later to serve as the Supreme Court's first black justice—concluded that it would take decades to effect real change by challenging segregation on a case-by-case basis. Instead, the decision was made to challenge the "separate but equal" doctrine of *Plessy v. Ferguson* head-on. *Brown v. Board of Education* was the result.

The NAACP lawyers' argument was simply this: segregated schools were inherently unequal and could not be made equal, and forcing blacks to attend such schools violated the constitutional guarantee of equal protection under law. The NAACP contended, through the testimony of social scientists, that segregation itself was the problem—no matter how good the buildings, teachers, and curriculum may be, segregation, by its very nature, diminished the self-esteem and educational development of black children.

The Supreme Court Rules . . . and Society Changes

The case was argued in the Supreme Court for a remarkable six days (usually, each side is limited to about an hour), and in a unanimous opinion brokered through the arduous efforts of Chief Justice Warren, the Supreme Court adopted the NAACP's position. "Segregation of white and colored children in public schools has a detrimental effect upon the colored children," the chief justice wrote in the Court's opinion, and the detriment is even "greater when it has the sanction of law; for the policy of segregating the races is usually interpreted as denoting the inferiority of the Negro group." Overruling more than a half century of precedent, Chief Justice Warren plainly stated that the doctrine of "separate but equal" has no place in American education—and, by implication, anywhere else in America.

But, having so ruled, the Court was left to decide what to do about segregated schools. Chief Justice Warren felt that he could not set a timetable for desegregation, and instead ruled that children must be admitted to public schools without regard for their race "with all deliberate speed." That now-famous phrase led to hundreds of local court challenges to desegregation measures in both the North and South, and even the use of federal troops to enforce local court desegregation decisions. But after enduring one of the most explosively divisive episodes in American history, by the early 1970s almost half of all black children in the South attended predominantly white schools—a higher percentage of desegregation than existed in the North.

As significant as the desegregation of public schools has proven to be, the reach of *Brown v. Board of Education* extends much further. The case sparked a firestorm of protests while at the same time creating much of the impetus for the Civil Rights Act of 1964; it spurred a string of later decisions that eliminated the legal underpinnings for other aspects of segregation in American life; and it laid much of the groundwork for the civil rights movement that continues through today. Many legal commentators consider Brown v. Board of Education to be the most significant Supreme Court decision of the twentieth century.

10. GRATZ v. BOLLINGER

11. GRUTTER v. BOLLINGER
Can One Race Be Favored Over Another Race in the Name of Diversity? 2003

Should your *race* ever matter?

In the 1990s, the University of Michigan utilized an admissions policy in its undergraduate school that assigned a predetermined number of points to various admissions criteria, such as grades, standardized test scores, quality of high school, residence, legacy status, and so on: the higher the point total, the greater the chance that an applicant would be admitted. The university wished to increase the diversity of its student population in order to serve its educational objectives and, therefore, it also added points to an applicant's admissions score if the applicant were a member of certain minority or racial groups that were underrepresented on campus. As the system existed in 1999, applicants who were members of these minority or racial groups would receive twenty extra points. This was significant—applicants with at least one hundred points were automatically admitted.

At about the same time, the University of Michigan Law School also sought to achieve diversity in its student body. However, in its admission process, the law school did not use a points system. Rather, it considered the usual factors (grades, standardized tests, recommendations, and so on), and also a variety of subjective and nontraditional criteria, one of which being whether the applicant would increase diversity. The law school did not limit its diversity goals to race or ethnicity—it also sought, for instance, geographic and economic diversity—but it did admit that it actively sought a "critical mass" of minority students.

Two well-qualified white Michigan residents who were denied admission as undergraduates, and one well-qualified white Michigan resident who was denied admission to the law school, filed suit against the university's president, claiming that they had been discriminated against on the basis of their race in violation of the Constitution and the Civil Rights Act of 1964. Ultimately, in 2003, the cases ended up in the Supreme Court: *Gratz v. Bollinger* and *Grutter v. Bollinger*.

The Supreme Court's Balancing Act

The issue involved the collision of two worthy goals. One goal was the avoidance of racism in any form. As a fundamental, bedrock principle, discrimination on the basis of race is unlawful. In America, we are to be judged by our qualifications, not our color. The other goal was diversification in our educational institutions. For all sorts of reasons, going as far back as *Brown v. Board of Education*, the Supreme Court agreed with the educators, sociologists, and other experts who concluded that "separate but equal" does not work, and diverse student bodies foster excellence in education.

But how can you increase diversity in a student body without considering the race of those you are considering for admission into the student body?

The Supreme Court justices were bitterly divided over how best to balance these competing goals. Rather than speaking in one voice, the vote was split, and even those justices who agreed on the result wrote separate opinions expressing different rationales. But out of this confusion, a portentous message emerged.

In the case of the University of Michigan undergraduate school, the Court found the admissions procedure to be unconstitutional, by a 6-3 margin. Any consideration of race must be very narrowly tailored, the Court ruled, and automatically awarding points for minority status was analogous to a quota system, and was over the line.

But in the case of the University of Michigan Law School, the Court ruled otherwise, although by only a 5-4 margin. It found that by reviewing each student individually (and less mechanically), and by crediting diversity factors aside from just race, the racial aspects of the admissions criteria had been sufficiently narrowed to satisfy constitutional requirements.

Color Blind No More?

This conclusion is of monumental significance. A majority of the Court crossed what had been a virtually impenetrable racial divide: the Supreme Court ruled that color blindness is no longer legally mandated in America, and that racial favoritism (the other side of which is racial discrimination) *can* be legal when narrowly undertaken in pursuit of a compelling goal.

The remaining issue is how this ruling can be taken. Could it be used to legalize certain kinds of racial discrimination?

Justice O'Connor, who wrote the majority opinion in the University of Michigan Law School case, justified her conclusion, at least in part, on the basis of practical considerations. Justice O'Connor observed that "American businesses have made clear that the skills needed in today's increasingly global marketplace can only be developed through exposure to widely diverse people, cultures, ideas, and viewpoints." It is not difficult to imagine the arguments this logic will lead to in the future. If race can be used as a university admissions criterion in order to serve the practical purpose of helping the university achieve its goals, why can't it be used as a business hiring criterion for the practical purpose of helping a business achieve *its* goals? For instance, if a company does business in Asia and will be more successful with its Asian customers and suppliers if it employs more Asian executives and salespeople, can it favor Asians over whites in the hiring process? And, ultimately, if an American company does business mainly with foreign companies who favor whites, could that be used by the American company as a justification to favor whites over minorities in its hiring process?

Having now created these issues, the Supreme Court will likely begin to resolve them in the coming years as more litigants test the boundaries of the *Gratz* and *Grutter* decisions. Whether this opens a floodgate, or merely a faucet, remains to be seen.

12. BOYS SCOUTS OF AMERICA v. DALE

Can Clubs and Associations be forced to admit gays, women, and minorities? 2000

James Dale, a college student, was a Boy Scout since he was twelve. He applied for a scoutmaster position, and was accepted. Shortly thereafter, Dale openly acknowledged that he was gay, and after a newspaper wrote an article featuring Dale's involvement in a gay rights group, the Boy Scouts of America revoked his membership, based on his sexual orientation.

Truly private clubs can usually admit, or not admit, who they want. But in many cases organizations that are generally open to the public are treated differently. In the case of New Jersey, like many states it had enacted a statute prohibiting discrimination on the basis of sexual orientation (among other characteristics, such as race and religion) by establishments (like restaurants and office buildings) and organizations (like the Boy Scouts) that usually admit just about anyone who walks through the door.

Dale sued the Boy Scouts, claiming that his rights under the New Jersey law had been violated. The Boy Scouts, on the other hand, argued that the New Jersey law violated its constitutional rights. We are entitled to our own standards and preferences, the Boy Scouts argued, and no state should have the right to tell us what to do about our own membership.

The Boy Scouts won in the trial court, but Dale won an appeal to the New Jersey Supreme Court. The Boy Scouts then appealed to the Supreme Court, resulting in the case of *Boy Scouts of America v. Dale*.

The Freedom Not to Associate

In prior cases, the Supreme Court ruled that even in the face of anti-discrimination statutes like New Jersey's, certain types of otherwise open-door associations do have a right to restrict their membership in certain circumstances. The First Amendment guarantees the people the freedom to associate with whomever they please. But, said the Court, there is also a freedom not to associate, even in the face of a contrary law, among certain kinds of groups. The Supreme Court calls these groups "expressive associations," meaning associations that promote certain values or points of view, like an association that promotes good citizenship or the importance of buying American-made goods. In that kind of a group, said the Court, the members' First Amendment rights of free speech could be compromised if the government were permitted to force them to accept people who opposed what the group stood for: picture an association whose mission is to promote unionization being forced to admit members who are anti-union.

But there are limits to how exclusive such expressive associations may be. In 1984, the Supreme Court decided a case, *Roberts v. Jaycees*, that explained how these conflicts are to be analyzed and resolved.

The *Roberts* case involved the Jaycees, or Junior Chamber of Commerce, a national civic organization that, at the time, restricted full voting membership to males between the ages of eighteen to thirty-five. Minnesota had an anti-discrimination law similar to New Jersey's, and a lawsuit was brought against the Jaycees seeking to invalidate the male-only policy.

The majority of the Supreme Court justices felt that the

Jaycees were an expressive association, but the Jaycees lost anyway, and were required to admit women. The rationale for the Supreme Court's decision was simple: admitting women into the Jaycees would not compromise the free speech rights of the Jaycees' membership, because the admission of women had nothing to do with the Jaycees' mission or message. The Jaycees promoted, for instance, community service and the development of business skills, and they could do just as good a job discussing and promoting those messages if women were members. Because the Jaycees' free speech rights would not be affected by enforcing the Minnesota law against it, the Supreme Court ruled that the Jaycees were required to abide by the law.

Dale argued that the same logic should apply to the Boy Scouts. Dale was more than qualified to be a scoutmaster, and he firmly believed in everything the Boy Scouts stood for. The fact that he happened to be gay, he argued, should have no more relevance than if he were black.

Unlike the Jaycees, however, the Boy Scouts won its case, although by only a 5-4 vote, and were permitted to exclude Dale solely because of his sexual orientation. Chief Justice Rehnquist wrote the opinion for the majority.

Rehnquist found that, like the Jaycees, the Boy Scouts was an expressive association entitled to First Amendment protection because it sought to transfer faith-based values, such as those in the Scout Oath and Scout Law, from adult members to youth members. Those values stressed the importance of being "morally straight" and "clean," and the Boy Scouts argued, without proof and based solely on the views of the organization's leadership, that homosexuals were not role models consistent with those precepts. If forced to allow homosexuals to serve as scoutmasters, the Boy Scouts contended, it would be forced to implicitly endorse a point of view with which it did not agree.

At the same time, however, the Boy Scouts admitted that none of the values it promoted mentioned anything about sexual orientation, and it had no evidence that gays in general, or Dale in particular, would do anything to interfere with the teaching of the Scout Oath or Scout Law. The Boy Scouts' case depended solely on its *opinion* about homosexuality in general: in the view of the Boy Scouts, merely *being* a homosexual was inconsistent with morality.

Rehnquist ruled that the Boy Scouts was entitled to its opinion. While stressing that the Supreme Court was not endorsing or agreeing with the Boy Scouts' view, Rehnquist concluded that it was not up to the Court to dictate what positions the Boy Scouts should espouse. Under the First Amendment, he ruled, the Boy Scouts could not be compelled to accept a scoutmaster if, in the Boy Scouts' view, the message the organization wanted to send to its members would be compromised.

The Dangers in Rehnquist's Ruling

Apart from the question of whether the Boy Scouts could be compelled to accept a gay scoutmaster, the dissent pointed out some disturbing implications of Rehnquist's opinion. The case was not just about whether the Boy Scouts should admit gays; it was about whether the Boy Scouts had the obligation, like everyone else, to obey a state law that prohibited discrimination against gays. The Boy Scouts were allowed to violate this law based solely on the opinion of the Boy Scouts' leadership that homosexuality was inherently immoral. When you are talking about allowing an organization to violate an otherwise valid law, the dissent argued, shouldn't it take more than just that?

Suppose the Jaycees had taken the position that, in its opinion, women are not civic minded and, therefore, their mere presence would negate the message the Jaycees tried to promote to its membership? Would the Jaycees have been permitted to exclude women on that rationale, without any evidence? What if an expressive organization that promotes business ethics refused to accept foreigners because, in the bigoted opinion of the organization's leaders, all foreigners are unethical?

The *Boy Scouts* decision has been criticized by many commentators of varying political leanings because of the ease with which it seems to allow an organization to engage in discriminatory conduct that is specifically prohibited by a state anti-discrimination statute. Cases that provoke this kind of controversy usually provoke more cases of the same type, and it would not be surprising if the Supreme Court took the opportunity to clarify the boundaries of the *Boy Scouts* ruling in the near future.

Chapter 5:
Playing Politics

*"Politics are too serious a matter to
be left to the politicians."*
—Charles de Gaulle,
former president of France

Democracies gather legitimacy from the free and fair elections through which they choose their leaders. History documents that if the electoral process loses credibility, the fabric of a democracy quickly unravels. It follows that a responsible government must focus, almost above all else, on preserving the public's confidence in the bona fides of its elections.

Increasingly, however, Americans have come to believe that elections can be bought, not by (as in prior eras) paying voters to stuff the ballot box, but through the purchase of media time and campaign machinery in such quantities as will steamroller an opponent of lesser means. The Supreme Court has recognized the dangers in a money-based electoral process, and the task of finding solutions that are both workable and constitutional has just begun.

There are other powers, as well, that the Supreme Court can use to assure the sanctity of our elections—as it attempted to do, with horrifically mixed reviews, in the 2000 presidential election.

13. BUCKLEY v. VALEO

*Money Talks: Campaign Finance Reform and the
First Amendment 1976*

From 1989 to 2002, Enron and its employees gave almost
$6 million in contributions to federal candidates and
parties. Did it get anything for its money? That depends on
who you ask, but there is no denying that Enron officials
had remarkable access to a sizeable array of elected and
appointed officials; a great deal of the energy policies and
legislation it sought were enacted; and persons that Enron
touted to the government as good candidates to populate
the agencies that regulated Enron often ended up in office.

Maybe the contributions had nothing to do with Enron's
political success. But there is at least a rational reason to
wonder whether they did—that is, whether government is
for sale to big money interests—and many feel that such
doubts and suspicions can be cancerous to the credibility a
democratic government requires. And the cancer may be
spreading, as the news media unravels story after story of
campaign contributions that, it is charged, bought special-
interest legislation for those who could afford to pay the
price.

Scandals like Enron have fueled the fight for campaign
finance reform. It is up to Congress to determine what type
of federal campaign finance reform, if any, is best for the
country, but there is a catch. Before Congress may rationally approach that issue, it has to confront a monumental
impediment—the Constitution.

All agree that political candidates have a First
Amendment right of free speech to get their message out to
as wide an audience as they can. In today's world, that

means using the mass media, and that takes money. The constitutional issue that has plagued campaign finance reform is whether the government can lawfully stop people who support the message a candidate is trying to publicize from providing the candidate with the money needed to do the job. Isn't the First Amendment all about the right of the people to join together and speak out on issues of public importance?

The Buckley Decision: Hush, Money

In the case of *Buckley v. Valeo*, the Supreme Court tried to answer that question. The case was brought by a senatorial odd couple—conservative Senator James Buckley and liberal Senator Eugene McCarthy—to challenge a federal campaign law that regulated campaign contributions.

The Court ruled that the First Amendment does invalidate laws that restrict a candidate from spending however much of his own money he wants to spend on his own election. In that context, said the Court, the money is closely tied to free speech because only by spending money can the candidate effectively communicate with the voters. If Ross Perot wants to spend $50 million on a presidential run, said the Court, more power to him.

But, said the majority in the *Buckley* Court, the same is not true in respect to political contributions, and the government *can* limit the amount of those contributions without offending the Constitution. Drawing a distinction many analysts believe to be logically nonexistent, the majority of the Court reasoned that contributions are not speech, even though most candidates cannot effectively speak without them and, therefore, contributions are not entitled to First Amendment protection.

There was, and still is, substantial disagreement among the justices regarding that proposition. For instance, Justice Thomas, writing in another case, put it succinctly: "A contribution, by amplifying the voice of the candidate, helps to ensure the dissemination of the messages that the contributor wishes to convey . . . By depriving donors of their right to speak through the candidate, contribution limits relegate donors' points of view to less effective modes of communication."

Buckley's Offspring: McCain-Feingold

Buckley broke the First Amendment ice for campaign finance reform, but it included a major loophole: in dealing only with the issue of contributions made directly to a candidate, it implicitly permitted the type of contribution which came to be known as "soft money." Instead of contributing directly to a candidate, a contributor would make the check payable to a political party or an organization which, for instance, would fund television ads that would run incessantly during a hotly contested political campaign. Not coincidentally, the ads would focus on an issue that distinguished one candidate from the other in the campaign and, without mentioning names, one candidate would be boosted over the other through the expenditure of millions of dollars which, if given directly to the favored candidate, would be starkly illegal.

To attack that loophole, Senators McCain and Feingold sponsored and successfully passed massive legislation, colloquially known as McCain-Feingold, but formally titled the "Bipartisan Campaign Reform Act" or "BCRA." BCRA seriously restricted "soft money" contributions, and fomented a well-funded, well-lawyered court challenge sponsored by a massive coalition of plaintiffs, and pursued in the name of Senator Mitch McConnell.

In the 2003 case of *McConnell v. FEC*, in a near-three hundred-page opinion supported by a bare 5-4 majority, the Supreme Court upheld (with minor exceptions) the constitutionality of BCRA. *Buckley* had opened a First Amendment door through which Senators McCain and Feingold escaped.

In the *McConnell* decision, the justices acknowledged that the country's method of electing candidates through massive infusions of interest group money created the appearance, and often the reality, of corruption. A substantial number of commentators who make their living parsing Supreme Court decisions explain the McConnell decision this way: the majority of the justices felt that they had to find a way, any way, around the First Amendment in order to allow campaign finance reform to move forward.

The *McConnell* dissenters were unrelenting and defiant. Justice Scalia wrote that the ruling was "a sad day for freedom of speech." "Who could have imagined," he said, "the Court would smile with favor upon a law that cuts to the heart of what the First Amendment is meant to protect: the right to criticize the government." Justice Thomas was even more condemnatory: "The Court today upholds what can only be described as the most significant abridgments of the freedom of speech and association since the Civil War."

Buckley, followed by *McConnell*, might change the way Americans choose their elected officials. But it might not. The issue is far from dead, and those on both sides continue to fight the fight with remarkable zeal. While *Buckley* established the general proposition that campaign contributions can be limited, cases now pending raise the issue of how far those limitations can be taken, and whom those limitations may affect. And many believe that as the roster of Supreme Court justices changes, a new majority may quickly jettison the *Buckley* framework altogether.

The Supreme Court itself acknowledged in *McConnell* that those persons and organizations with the money and will to support political positions will continue to fund the fight to make their money talk. As the majority in the *McConnell* decision wrote, "We are under no illusion that BCRA—the Bipartisan Campaign Reform Act—will be the last congressional statement on the matter. Money, like water, will always find an outlet."

14. BUSH v. GORE

Did the Supreme Court Play Politics in the 2000 Election? 2000

In the view of many, the Supreme Court elected George W. Bush the president of the United States.

After the ballots were counted in the November 7, 2000, presidential election, Gore led Bush in the popular vote, and Gore led the electoral college vote by a 267/246 margin. Whoever reached 270 electoral college votes would win the presidency. The only state still in play was Florida, whose 25 electoral votes would go to the candidate who won the Florida popular vote. The initial Florida vote count had Bush leading Gore, 2,909,135 votes to 2,907,351, but because the margin was less than 0.5 percent, Florida law required a machine recount. The machine recount reduced Bush's margin to a scant 327 votes.

Gore, as was his right, then requested a manual recount in four Florida counties. Florida law, however, mandated that the recount be completed in seven days. This led three of the counties to request more time to complete the manual recount, but Florida's secretary of state, Katherine Harris, believing that an extension would be unlawful, refused the request. Gore disagreed with Harris's position, filed a lawsuit, and the legal dispute that eventually became *Bush v. Gore* was born.

In short order, Gore's case was argued before the Florida Supreme Court, which issued an order requiring Harris to allow the requested extension, through November 26. Bush appealed that ruling to the Supreme Court, which requested certain clarifications before it would rule. In the interim, one of the counties, Miami-Dade, canceled its manual recount, stating that it could not complete the recount by the November 26 deadline.

On November 26, despite the incomplete recount, Harris certified Bush as the winner by only 537 votes—thereby awarding Bush Florida's 25 electoral votes, and the presidency.

On November 27, Gore filed another suit to contest the certified results of the election. He lost, and again appealed to the Florida Supreme Court which, on December 8, ordered a state-wide, manual recount. Bush again appealed to the U.S. Supreme Court, which issued an injunction stopping the statewide recount, pending its final decision.

On December 11, the Supreme Court heard oral arguments. Just sixteen hours later, with the presidency in the balance and the nation on the edge of its seat, the Court rendered its opinion.

Hanging Chads, Dimpled Chads, and Equal Protection

The Supreme Court tied most of its analysis to the Equal Protection Clause of the Fourteenth Amendment to the Constitution, which provides that, "No State shall . . . deny to any person . . . the equal protection of the laws." In the wake of televised accounts of election commissioners squinting through magnifying glasses, some finding significance in "hanging chads," others being influenced by "dimpled chads," Bush argued that there was no uniform vote-counting standard among the various Florida counties and, therefore, two voters in different counties could mark their ballots in an identical manner, and one would be counted while the other would be disregarded. This, said Bush, was a denial of equal protection, and the recount should be halted on that basis.

Gore argued that equal protection does not require absolute uniformity, and because all of the Florida counties subscribed to one standard—trying to derive the intent of the voters who marked the ballots—the Equal Protection Clause was satisfied. Gore pointed out that every state uses a variety of different methods to record votes in different counties, ranging from optical scanners to punch cards. Therefore, said Gore, if Bush prevailed, from that day forward every state would have to implement a uniform system of voting in order to satisfy constitutional standards, which was neither required under the law, nor possible as a matter of stark reality.

The Supreme Court's decision was a hodgepodge of arcane legal reasoning and varying alliances among varying justices on varying points, but the upshot was that Bush won. Essentially, the majority of justices ruled that the different vote-counting techniques undertaken in the recount were constitutionally problematic. This meant that the manual recount had to cease, and the election results had to be certified as they existed prior to the recount. Bush assumed the presidency on the strength of that opinion.

The Criticism From Without, and From Within

Bush v. Gore touched off an immediate explosion of political commentary although, not surprisingly, in most instances those politicians who favored the Court's reasoning were prior adherents of Bush or his philosophies, and vice versa.

In addition, constitutional law scholars quickly emerged from their ivory towers. While some supported the decision, those who garnered the most media attention vituperatively denounced the legal underpinnings of the *Bush v. Gore* decision, often charging that the justices voted their politics, and not the law. American University law professor Jamin Raskin wrote in the *Washington Monthly* that *Bush v. Gore* was "quite demonstrably the worst Supreme Court decision in history," even worse than the infamous *Dred Scott* decision. Harvard law professor Laurence Tribe, one of the country's most respected constitutional scholars (and one of the attorneys who represented Gore), wrote that the Court's opinion "cannot be grounded in any previously recognizable form of equal protection doctrine." Another Harvard law professor, Randall Kennedy, labeled the decision a "hypocritical mishmash of ideas." Mincing no words on his view of why the majority ruled as it did, Sanford Levinson, a University of Texas law professor, wrote in *The Nation* that the decision was "easily explainable" as the decision of Republican justices intended "to assure the triumph of a fellow Republican who might not become president if Florida were left to its own legal process."

Perhaps most disturbing, however, was the fact that allegations of this type, charging nothing short of judicial corruption, were not limited to pundits and professors. In divisive matters of national importance that consume the nation's attention, the Supreme Court strives for a unanimous opinion in the effort to speak with one voice and promote national unity. When, as in *Bush v. Gore*, that cannot be achieved, Supreme Court justices will normally characterize their disagreements as good faith disputes over legal precedents or philosophy. Very rarely will they question each other's motives or integrity. In *Bush v. Gore,* however, Justice Stevens, one of the dissenters, used startling language to characterize his view of what the Court's majority had done. He wrote that the majority's position can only lend credence to the most cynical appraisal of the work of judges throughout the land. It is confidence in the men and women who administer the judicial system that is the true backbone of the rule of law. Time will one day heal the wound to that confidence that will be inflicted by today's decision. One thing, however, is certain. Although we may never know with complete certainty the identity of the winner of this year's Presidential election, the identity of the loser is perfectly clear. It is the Nation's confidence in the judge as an impartial guardian of the rule of law.

In advance of the 2004 presidential election, many had predicted that whoever lost would challenge the results based on the *Bush v. Gore* ruling that disparate vote-counting procedures could violate the Equal Protection Clause, and that the nation would then be thrown into tumult. Obviously, that did not happen. It is certainly forseeable, however, that another too-close-to-call vote could emerge in a future election, resulting in a similar lawsuit. Especially in view of the changing makeup of the Court since 2000, it is impossible to predict whether the Supreme Court will again delve into the electoral process, or instead leave it to the states to untangle their own messes (as the dissenting justices argued the Court should have done in 2000). In making that future decision, the then-sitting justices will, no doubt, be mindful of the firestorm *Bush v. Gore* ignited, and it would not be surprising if, at that time, the Court looked for a way out, instead of a way in.

Whether *Bush v. Gore* will cause the American people to

doubt the ostensibly apolitical nature of the Supreme Court in the future will likely depend on how the post-2000 appointees to the Court acquit themselves in the public eye. If future decisions are perceived as exercises in which they strain to reach results that conform with their known predispositions, that will lead to one type of public perception, and comparisons to *Bush v. Gore* will be inevitable. If those decisions reflect objectivity and legal scholarship that lead to results that support no particular political or policy point of view, the questions engendered by *Bush v. Gore* will likely be viewed as having only historical significance.

Chapter 6
The Right of Privacy: From Before the Cradle to the Grave

"The right to be let alone is indeed the beginning of all freedom."
—William O. Douglas,
Supreme Court justice, 1939–1975

Justice Douglas was a staunch supporter of individual rights, but as even he would concede, the yearning to be let alone must have its limits. As Justice Oliver Wendell Holmes Jr. put it, "The right to swing my fist ends where the other man's nose begins."

Still, Justice Holmes's commonsense rule creates its own conundrum: it is not always so easy to determine just where the other man's figurative nose really is.

Sometimes, of course, the line is obvious—you can't steal money or pollute a river. But what about when an individual minds his own business, but chooses to live his private life in a way that violates the majority's principles or sensibilities? Does the law have the right to tell you what you are allowed to do in your own house, or with your own body, or with your own family?

15. GRISWOLD v. CONNECTICUT

The Unwritten Right of Privacy 1965

In *Griswold v. Connecticut*, the Supreme Court found within the Constitution a new and fundamental right: the right of privacy. In the process, the Supreme Court created the legal foundation on which, eight years later, *Roe v. Wade* was built, and on which other, as yet unforeseen judicial results may also be founded. In addition, the *Griswold* case set off a conflagration, which continues through today, over the proper role of a Supreme Court justice in American society.

The background for the *Griswold* case goes back to 1879, when Connecticut passed a law outlawing contraception, and making it a crime to use, or to assist or counsel anyone to use, "any drug, medicinal article or instrument for the purpose of preventing conception." The law was almost never enforced, but many persons found it an offensive intrusion into their personal lives, and wanted it off the books.

In the effort to create a test case to challenge the constitutionality of the law, Estelle Griswold, executive director of the Planned Parenthood League of Connecticut, and Dr. C. Lee Buxton, a physician and professor at Yale School of Medicine, opened a birth control clinic in New Haven. Shortly thereafter, they were arrested, tried, found guilty, and fined $100. They appealed, and the Supreme Court eventually agreed to hear their case.

Constitution or Conscience?

Sometimes, a judge is presented with a case where justice and common sense cry out for a particular result—but there's no obvious law that allows the judge to get where he desperately wants to go. *Griswold* was that type of case. The vast majority of citizens, and all of the Supreme Court justices involved in *Griswold*, felt that the Connecticut law was an absurd and even repugnant invasion of the lives of married couples. Yet there was no apparent constitutional hook on which to hang the argument that the Connecticut statute was invalid.

Some justices, when faced with that kind of a case, view their sworn role as being limited to the enforcement of the Constitution as written, no matter the unfairness that may result in a particular situation. Their rationale is that if we are to remain a "government of laws and not men," some injustices may have to be suffered in order to avoid a greater evil—the creation of a judiciary in which justices are free to make up the law as they go along in order to dispense their own brands of situational equity.

Other justices, however, view their role much differently. They view the law in general, and the Constitution in particular, as a living, evolving rule book that has to change as society changes, and as new, unforeseen situations are presented. They acknowledge an obligation to stay as close as feasible to the intent of the Constitution as written, but they view it as their duty to stretch its language in order to do what justice requires.

Penumbras and Emanations

Justice Douglas wrote the majority opinion in *Griswold*. He was an individualist who enthusiastically subscribed to the view that the law should be expanded when required to protect individual rights.

Justice Douglas conceded that the word "privacy" appears

nowhere in the Constitution. Nevertheless, he concluded that, at least insofar as married couples are concerned, a fundamental right of privacy is implicit in the various guarantees given in the Bill of Rights, which is comprised of the first ten amendments to the Constitution. In some of the most famous (and ridiculed) language ever written by a Supreme Court justice, he offered that "the Bill of Rights have penumbras, formed by emanations from those guarantees that help give them life and substance." For instance, the Fourth Amendment precludes unreasonable searches and seizures, which implies a right of privacy. The Fifth Amendment gives citizens the right against self incrimination, which Justice Douglas likened to a personal "zone of privacy."

Two justices, Black and Stewart, held judicial philosophies vastly different than Douglas's, and dissented. Justice Black found the Connecticut law "offensive." Justice Stewart called it "uncommonly silly." But that alone, they wrote, did not make it unconstitutional. Justice Black went on, "The Court talks about a constitutional 'right of privacy' as though there is some constitutional provision or provisions forbidding any law ever to be passed which might abridge the privacy of individuals. But there is not." He concluded, "I like my privacy as well as the next one, but I am nevertheless compelled to admit that government has a right to invade it unless prohibited by some specific constitutional provision."

Griswold's Unintended Consequences

Griswold is extremely important, for at least two reasons: what the justices said in the case; and what the Justices did in the case.

Concerning what was said in *Griswold*, by creating a new and fundamental right of privacy, *Griswold* provided a means for future Supreme Court justices to reach ends that were previously unreachable. The prime example is, of course, *Roe v. Wade*. In addition, however, *Griswold* was used as the legal justification for the Court to strike down laws barring the sale of contraceptives to unmarried couples in 1972; in 2003, in the case of *Lawrence v. Texas*, the Supreme Court, building on *Griswold* without really admitting it, declared unconstitutional a state sodomy law and in the process invalidated all laws seeking to regulate intimate contact among adults.

Concerning what was done in *Griswold*, those who believe that the Constitution must be broadly interpreted to adjust to changing times were heartened, and those who believe that the Constitution must be strictly construed according to its language or, at most, the known intent of the framers, were outraged. Thanks in large part to *Griswold*, the judicial school of thought favored by a prospective justice has become a near-litmus test for those nominated to the Supreme Court. In their Senate confirmation hearings, prospective justices are routinely asked if they believe in a constitutional right to privacy. This is code for a question that asks, in one sense, if they would interpret the Constitution broadly or strictly and, in another sense, if they might consider reversing *Roe v. Wade*.

16. ROE v. WADE

Does the Right of Privacy Include the Right to an Abortion? 1973

Roe v. Wade is one of the most vigorously debated and politically sensitive Supreme Court decisions in American history. It arose out of a Texas statute that, like statutes in many other states, prohibited abortions except for the medical purpose of saving the mother's life. Roe, an unmarried pregnant woman who sought an abortion, filed a lawsuit in which she claimed the statute was unconstitutional, and the case was ultimately heard by the Supreme Court.

Roe won her case. Justice Blackmun, joined by six other justices, ruled that the Constitution permits a woman to decide for herself whether to terminate her pregnancy, although the state could regulate abortion procedures in order to safeguard the woman's health and maintain medical standards. It is only when the fetus becomes able to live outside the womb, the Court ruled, that states may prohibit abortions, except those abortions required to preserve the life or health of the mother.

The fact that the justices were passionately at odds over *Roe*, and remain so, is well known. Justice White, among others, wrote a withering dissent. "I find nothing in the language or history of the Constitution to support the Court's judgment . . . its judgment is an improvident and extravagant exercise of the power of judicial review that the Constitution extends to this Court." Justice Rehnquist wrote that the *Roe* majority based their decision on a supposed right that was "completely unknown" to the drafters of the Constitution.

In particular, two aspects of *Roe v. Wade* continue to stir wide-ranging fervor and controversy.

First, the Court refused to rule that, under the Constitution, an unborn child is a "person" entitled to constitutional protections. *Roe* is largely responsible for the raging political debate over when life begins, even though it failed to make a meaningful attempt to engage in the debate it created.

Second, the Court based much of its logic on a "right to privacy" that prior cases (like the *Griswold v. Connecticut* decision discussed earlier) found to exist within the Constitution, even though no such right is set forth in the Constitution in so many words. Using *Griswold* and similar cases as a legal steppingstone, *Roe* expanded the newfound right to privacy "to encompass a woman's decision whether or not to terminate her pregnancy." Many commentators find the notion that the Constitution includes a fundamental right of privacy to be more fabrication than interpretation, and they further find the extension of that supposed right to abortion to be a logical and moral non sequitur. Others, of course, vehemently disagree.

Roe's Future, and the Future of Abortion

Despite the ongoing controversy, *Roe's* central holding—that a woman has a right to an abortion up until the time the fetus is viable—has stood the test of time. The Court has struck down restrictions it deemed to unreasonably compromise the right to an abortion, such as state laws requiring a woman to obtain the consent of her husband. In 1992, in *Planned Parenthood v. Casey*, the Court reaffirmed its commitment to *Roe* and, while signaling that it would accept certain restrictions on the right to an abortion, it made plain that it would invalidate any restrictions that placed "an undue burden" on the right of a woman to obtain an abortion before the fetus attains viability.

The fate of *Roe* in either the long term or the short term is anything but certain. As the makeup of the Court changes, the odds for the reversal of *Roe* change as well. Whether *Roe's* expansion of the constitutional right of privacy signals a trend, or comprises an aberration, may well depend on whether future presidents choose Supreme Court nominees who favor a strict or broad reading of the Constitution. This much is certain: abortion opponents will continue to test *Roe*, and the Supreme Court will have an ongoing flow of cases through which to expand, constrict, or reverse *Roe*.

But there is a common misconception that if *Roe* is reversed, abortion will be illegal. That's just not so. A ban on abortion would require a monumental shift in constitutional law, and perhaps a constitutional amendment.

Roe ruled that a state statute prohibiting abortion is unconstitutional; if *Roe* is reversed, states will be permitted, as they were before *Roe*, to outlaw abortion—but states will also have the right, as they did before *Roe*, *not* to outlaw abortion. The upshot will likely be a political maelstrom of activity in state legislatures across the country, including a variety of ballot initiatives and referenda, all of which will lead to a regulatory crazy quilt in which some states allow abortion and other states prohibit abortion.

Still, for some women, the reversal of *Roe* could, as a practical matter, eliminate their ability to obtain an abortion: if they live in a state where abortion is illegal, health or financial constraints may make it impossible for them to travel to another state, particularly if adjoining states enact lengthy residency requirements as a way to avoid becoming abortion havens.

The debate specifically over *Roe* is not, therefore, a debate over whether abortion should be legal or illegal, as much as it is a debate over whether the ability to obtain an abortion should be made easier or more difficult, or should be made to depend on a woman's financial circumstances, or should be made to depend on geography.

17. WASHINGTON V. GLUCKSBERG
The Right to Die 1997

Suppose a close friend becomes terminally ill, all quality of life has evaporated, and he is suffering. Moreover, his medical bills will dissipate his assets, and he is desperately worried about his family's financial future. He tells you he would prefer to die—peacefully, without pain, now. He pleads with you, as his closest friend, to help him carry out his wishes. All you need to do is fill an old painkiller prescription he has, give him the bottle, and he will do the rest. May you do it? May you arrange for a doctor or nurse to help him, and even if you could, would they be permitted to do anything?

As of this writing, forty-nine states prohibit assisted suicide, and in recent years doctors, terminally ill patients, and "death with dignity" organizations have challenged the constitutionality of these laws in court. One such challenge was mounted in the mid-1990s by Dr. Harold Glucksberg, along with other physicians, patients, and a nonprofit advocacy group. It involved a Washington state statute that makes "promoting a suicide" a felony. Glucksberg sought the right to honor the wishes of terminal patients who asked for his assistance. The case, *Washington v. Glucksberg*, made its way to the Supreme Court in 1997.

The Limits of Liberty

Glucksberg, like most litigants who have challenged assisted suicide bans, based his case on the historic Due Process Clause of the Fourteenth Amendment, which prohibits a state from depriving persons of "life, liberty, or property without due process of law." Surely, Glucksberg contended, this constitutional right of liberty must include the right of a competent adult to choose to die, and to seek assistance in implementing that decision. As the saying goes, it's a free country.

Some lower courts had agreed with this argument in other cases, but the Supreme Court, in an opinion written by Chief Justice Rehnquist, unanimously disagreed. The Court found that the Due Process Clause does not prevent government from regulating all conceivable liberties, but only certain *fundamental* liberties rooted in the nation's history and traditions. The Court reviewed Anglo-American law since the 1400s, and found that England, and then the colonies, had prohibited assisted suicides for hundreds of years. Therefore, the Court ruled, there was no reason to believe that the framers of the Constitution intended to contravene this tradition and establish a "right to die." Consequently, said the Court, it was not unconstitutional for a state to criminalize assisted suicide.

Keep in mind, however, that while *Washington v. Glucksberg* stands for the proposition that states may lawfully prohibit assisted suicides within their borders, states may also allow assisted suicides if they wish. So far, Oregon is the only state to have done so, enacting the Death with Dignity Act, which became effective in 1997. The law permits physicians, in well-defined circumstances, to provide a lethal dosage of pills to terminally ill patients who seek to end their own suffering. It is then up to the patient to take the pills, or not. The Bush administration challenged the constitutionality of the Death with Dignity Act and, in January 2006, the Supreme Court, while not endorsing the law, refused to overturn it, in a 6-3 vote. Several other states were awaiting the outcome of this ruling, and will now likely introduce similar legislation.

As was the case with abortion before *Roe v. Wade* (and as will be the case if *Roe* is overruled), whether or not you have the right to die through assisted suicide will, for the foreseeable future, depend on where you live.

Chapter 7
"Big Government" in Your Business and Your Backyard

"Liberty implies the absence of arbitrary restraint, not immunity from reasonable regulations . . ."
—Justice Charles Evans Hughes

The venerated Due Process Clause of the Fourteenth Amendment prohibits the government from depriving any person "of life, liberty, or property, without due process of law." Stated differently, the government can take your property, your liberty, and even your life, so long as it goes about doing it in the right way.

This principle applies in a myriad of contexts, one of which is the world of commerce: just how far can the government go in restricting how people conduct business, or in regulating what happens on the job, or in deciding who wins the conflicts between business interests and individual rights?

The answer to these questions can be complex, implicating not only the Due Process Clause, but other constitutional provisions as well. Decades ago, the Supreme Court seemingly defined much of this legal landscape but, as will be seen, it may now be in the process of changing its mind in important ways, and where it ultimately ends up will have profound effects on the role of government in our society.

18. WEST COAST HOTEL CO. v. PARISH
What Gives Congress the Right to Regulate Private Businesses? 1937

In the early 1900s, state legislatures began to enact measures designed to protect workers, such as child labor laws, maximum hour laws, and workers compensation laws. The Supreme Court, however, quickly put the constitutional brakes on these efforts, setting the stage for a momentous power struggle and constitutional crisis decades later. The outcome of that struggle would determine not only whether Congress would be permitted to protect workers, but also whether it would be permitted to address the country's social issues, ranging from outlawing segregation to protecting the food supply.

The conflict began in earnest when New York enacted a law limiting the work week to sixty hours in certain industries. The law was challenged, and in 1905 the case, *Lochner v. New York*, worked its way to the Supreme Court. The Court's analysis in *Lochner* focused on the Due Process Clause of the Fourteenth Amendment to the Constitution: "No person shall be . . . deprived of life, liberty, or property, without due process of law." Central to this right, said the Court, was the liberty to enter into contracts without government interference, and that included contracts between employers and employees. Based on that logic, in a 5-4 decision the Court ruled that laws "limiting the hours in which grown and intelligent men may labor to earn their living" are "mere meddlesome interferences with the rights of the individual." The New York law was ruled unconstitutional. In effect, the Supreme

Court ruled that the government was obligated to leave businesses, and the people who worked for and dealt with businesses, to their own devices.

Roosevelt's Reaction: The "Court-Packing Plan"

Lochner remained unchallenged until Franklin D. Roosevelt and the "New Dealers" took power in the wake of the Great Depression. A fundamental part of Roosevelt's economic recovery plan was the implementation of health and safety codes. Court challenges to these codes predictably resulted, and in 1935, using the *Lochner* precedent, the Supreme Court began to dismantle what Roosevelt had done: it invalidated an act that allowed farmers to hold on to their farms during foreclosure; it invalidated minimum wage, maximum hour, and health codes in the poultry industry; and it invalidated Roosevelt's key agricultural reforms.

Roosevelt was beyond livid, and on February 5, 1937, he unveiled what came to be known as the "court-packing plan": Roosevelt sought to cajole Congress into passing a law that would allow him to appoint an extra Supreme Court justice for each present justice who was over seventy which, at that time, would increase the number of justices from nine to sixteen. Roosevelt's ostensible purpose was to assist older justices to carry the Court's workload, but his obvious intent was to gain control over a Court that he viewed as a dangerous impediment to economic recovery and social justice. Roosevelt lobbied hard for the legislation through vituperative attacks on the Court, back room deal-making, and nationally broadcast "fireside chats." While there was support for the plan in some quarters, there was substantial suspicion as well—if the president could, essentially, "rig" the Court to suit his purposes, what would become of the "check and balance" role the Supreme Court was to play in the Constitution's elegant plan?

Less than two months later, while Senate hearings on Roosevelt's plan were proceeding, the Supreme Court handed down a decision in the case of *West Coast Hotel Co. v. Parish*. The case involved a challenge to the constitutionality of the state of Washington's minimum wage laws. The Supreme Court had recently overturned similar laws by a 5-4 margin, and it was expected that the *West Coast Hotel* case would face the same fate.

The Switch in Time That Saved Nine

This time, however, the 5-4 majority went the other way—one of the justices, Justice Roberts, inexplicably switched his vote and signed on to an opinion authored by Chief Justice Hughes, who abandoned *Lochner* in favor of a rationale that became the foundation for national minimum wage laws, Social Security, the regulation of public utilities, agricultural quotas, and much more. Liberty, said the chief justice (along with his newfound colleague), be it freedom of contract or any other liberty, is not absolute, but can and must be regulated so that the citizenry may be protected against "the evils which menace the health, safety, morals, and welfare of the people."

This was sweet music to FDR's ears, and the confrontation between the executive and the judiciary quickly became a collaboration. Justice Roberts's change of heart was soon dubbed the "switch in time that saved nine." Historians have never been able to definitively establish whether Justice Roberts's turnabout was the result of the pressure exerted by Roosevelt on the Court, or an honest change in viewpoint but, in the years that followed, Roosevelt was able to implement the social legislation of the New Deal without further interference from the Supreme Court, and the congressional impetus to keep enacting such legislation continued for more than fifty years.

19. HEART OF ATLANTA HOTEL v. UNITED STATES

20. KATZENBACH v. MCCLUNG

What Are the Limits on Congress's Right to Regulate Business, and Beyond? 1964

The *West Coast Hotel* case cleared the way for Congress, whether on its own or at the urging of the president, to enact broad-brush business legislation that changed the way Americans live. But the decision raised two far-reaching questions.

First, does the federal government's right to regulate business stop at the national or, at worst, the industry level? Or can it also reach into local communities and regulate individual businesses? For instance, can the federal government dictate how much the corner store must pay its employees, or what hours it can operate? Or should issues like those be decided strictly on the community or, at worst, the state level?

Second, if the federal government is ultimately allowed to reach into local towns in order to tell businesses how to behave, is it also allowed to dictate what subjects must be taught in the local schools, and who the local police department is permitted to hire? Where does the power stop?

Much of the answer lies in a provision in the Constitution known as the "Commerce Clause," and the extent of the power that provision gives the federal government is now the subject of one of the hottest Supreme Court debates in decades. Two cases decided in the 1960s,

Heart of Atlanta Motel v. United States and *Katzenbach v. McClung*, took the pendulum about as far as it could go in one direction, but it now appears to be quickly swinging the other way.

Some background is necessary to understand how we got where we are, and where we may be going.

The Supreme Court Expands the Commerce Clause

In the years before the Constitution was created, the states were waging economic wars among themselves through protective tariffs and retaliatory trade regulations, making the creation of a national economy virtually impossible. This was one of the major reasons why the Founding Fathers convened a Constitutional Convention—the goal was to forge a federal government with sufficient power to create a workable system of national commerce. The so-called Commerce Clause of the Constitution was the result: it granted Congress the power "to Regulate Commerce with foreign nations, and among the Several States, and with the Indian Tribes."

In the early nineteenth century, Congress began to flex its federal muscles, and it enacted a variety of laws requiring that the states cease interference with interstate commerce so that a national economy might develop more quickly. For instance, it imposed interstate rail and shipping rates and practices so that one state could not, through its own laws, obtain an economic leg up on another state. When these laws were challenged as being beyond congressional authority, the Supreme Court ruled that, in fact, Congress had been empowered by the Commerce Clause to regulate interstate commerce, and it therefore had the right under the Constitution to take such actions.

Through the remainder of the nineteenth century and into the twentieth century, as industry expanded and the economy grew, Congress further amplified its legislative activities, and the businesses that bore the brunt of these regulations again challenged them in court. Often, the challenge was based on the fact that the activity Congress sought to regulate took place within just one state, as opposed to taking place in "interstate commerce." For instance, Congress passed laws regulating what occurred in stockyards, even though the stockyards were situated in only a single state.

The Supreme Court allowed these laws to stand by dramatically expanding the concept of "interstate commerce" to include economic activities that took place solely within one state, on the theory that such activities plainly affected commerce in other states. For example, it ruled that a stockyard located and doing business only in Chicago could nonetheless be regulated by Congress because the livestock in the stockyard were ultimately destined for shipment to states all over the country—that is, the stockyard was connected to an interstate distribution chain and was therefore itself in interstate commerce. Using this interpretation of "interstate commerce," the Court allowed Congress to implement legislation imposing workplace rules, establishing union rights, mandating payment for overtime, setting commodity prices, regulating strip mining, and controlling a host of other in-state economic activities, all on the theory that the activities "affected" interstate commerce, and were therefore authorized by the Commerce Clause.

Taking the Commerce Clause To, and Perhaps Beyond, the Limit

The Supreme Court's willingness to expand Congress's rights under the Commerce Clause reached a zenith in 1964. Congress passed the Civil Rights Act of 1964 to prohibit discrimination on the basis of race, color, religion, or national origin in places of public accommodation, like hotels and restaurants. Congress knew that its right to regulate private conduct of this type was questionable—the Civil Rights Act did not really focus on regulating economic activity in the same way that legislation affecting, for instance, stockyards and commodities did. It was plainly focused on ending discrimination, and nothing more. However, Congress inserted a provision stating that a facility was covered under the Act "if its operations affect commerce"—Congress hoped that the Supreme Court would use that language as a hook to rule that the Commerce Clause gave Congress the power it needed to do just about anything Congress wanted to do.

As expected, the Civil Rights Act of 1964 was immediately challenged in court. The Heart of Atlanta Motel, located in downtown Atlanta, insisted on continuing its practice of refusing to rent rooms to blacks. The motel was near a highway and served intrastate, as well was interstate travelers. Similarly, Ollie's Barbecue, a large restaurant in Birmingham, Alabama, insisted on continuing its practice of serving whites at tables, but providing only takeout service for blacks. It purchased some of its food—approximately $70,000 a year—from out-of-state suppliers, and served interstate travelers. The owners of both establishments argued that the Commerce Clause could not logically be used to give the federal government regulatory power over their businesses, which had only microscopic and indirect effects on interstate commerce.

The cases that resulted from these court challenges, *Heart of Atlanta Motel v. United States* and *Katzenbach v. McClung*, ultimately reached the Supreme Court—and in deciding those cases the Court upheld the power of Congress to enact the Civil Rights Act of 1964 pursuant to the authority granted by the Commerce Clause. These decisions were monumentally important: for better or worse, they validated Congress's right not only to fight racial discrimination throughout the country, but to reach into local towns and attack virtually all manner of social ills and wrongs through federal lawmaking. The body of social legislation that arose from Congress during the 1960s, 1970s and 1980s can in large measure be attributed to these decisions.

The rationale the Court used in the *Heart of Atlanta Motel* and *Katzenbach* cases stretched the words of the Commerce Clause to (and some say beyond) their limits. The Court reasoned that both businesses, even though they did not directly engage in interstate commerce, catered to people who themselves moved in interstate commerce, and it stood to reason that the cumulative effect of discriminating against a portion of those people affected interstate commerce in some substantial way. It was not necessary, said the Court, to engage in quantification efforts or detailed analyses—if it could be rationally concluded that the activities Congress was regulating had a material effect on interstate commerce, that was enough.

The Supreme Court's Retreat

Based on these Commerce Clause precedents, there was little that was beyond Congress's reach—and Congress took full advantage of its power, enacting federal legislation that affected innumerable aspects of local life. Critics complained that this distorted the Commerce Clause beyond its plain meaning, and gave Congress powers the Founding Fathers never intended it to have.

By 1995, however, a majority of the Supreme Court was comprised of justices who shared these critics' judicial philosophies, and the result has been a serious change in direction, with major implications.

It began with the 1995 case of *United States v. Lopez*. The Supreme Court addressed the constitutionality of the Gun-Free School Zones Act of 1990, in which Congress made it a federal offense for a person to possess a firearm in a school zone. The Act was challenged in court, and in a 5-4 decision handed down in 1995, the Supreme Court ruled that the regulation of guns in school zones did not involve a sufficient connection to economic activity to implicate the federal government's Commerce Clause powers, and the federal government was therefore legislating in a realm in which it had no authority. The decision floored most legal analysts, who had come to take the Commerce Clause for granted.

Five years later, in 2000, the Supreme Court did it again. In the case of *United States v. Morrison*, the Court faced a challenge to a federal law that prohibited violence against women. In another 5-4 decision, the Supreme Court ruled that the the law exceeded the federal government's power under the Commerce Clause. Even though violence against women may have economic implications that affect interstate commerce, the Court ruled that "crimes of violence are not, in any sense of the phrase, economic activity" and Congress was therefore not empowered under the Commerce Clause to legislate in that arena. *Lopez* was no longer an aberration; it appeared to be part of a trend.

In both cases, the four dissenting justices fervently pointed out that Congress had assembled evidence in reports and hearings establishing that violence in schools substantially affects the quality of education, and a lesser-educated workforce has an obvious affect on interstate commerce. Even more troubling, they reasoned, Congress had established a "mountain of data" assembled during four years of hearings documenting the substantial effects that violence against women has on the economy—far more than any evidence that supported the decisions in the *Heart of Atlanta Motel* and *Katzenbach* cases. The majority was unmoved.

These cases, and the whole idea of the Commerce Clause, may seem somewhat esoteric, but they raise a fundamental issue: what is the role of the federal government in solving the country's social problems? The law is plainly in flux, but the current Court may be bent on transferring a substantial degree of responsibility for social problems from the Capitol to the state houses and the town halls.

21. BURLINGTON INDUSTRIES V. ELLERTH

Expanding the Rights of Employees to Sue Their Employers 1998

Sometimes, it is the Supreme Court itself, not Congress, that multiplies the scope and effect of government regulation. Such was the case in the 1998 case of *Burlington Industries v. Ellerth*, where the Supreme Court, acting in the role of interpreting an Act of Congress, changed the rules of the American workplace, and made it much easier for employees to win sexual harassment and other lawsuits against their employers. The result has been a major increase in employee versus employer lawsuits, many ending in six- and seven-figure verdicts, and a radical shift in the way employers must manage their workforces.

Ellerth, a Burlington Industries salesperson, was subjected to constant sexual harassment from her supervisor. However, even though she knew that Burlington prohibited sexual harassment, she did not report her supervisor's misconduct, and she eventually quit. Ellerth then sued Burlington, claiming that the sexual harassment forced her to resign.

At the trial, Burlington proved that it had done all anyone could have reasonably expected it to do. It had established clear policies forbidding sexual harassment; it did not know about the sexual harassment that Ellerth had suffered; and absent a report from Ellerth, it had no realistic way of finding out about it. Burlington's defense was airtight: it was not negligent and, as a result, it should not he held liable for the unknown acts of a renegade supervisor who was furtively violating Burlington's policies. Burlington won the case in the trial court.

Ellerth filed an appeal, and ultimately the Supreme Court agreed to hear her case. Ellerth contended that the Supreme Court should change the law of sexual harassment by applying a legal doctrine well entrenched in other kinds of cases, known as "vicarious liability." If, for instance, a company's truck driver runs a red light and causes an accident, the law provides that the company is "vicariously liable" for the actions of its employee, whether or not the company was itself negligent. The same would be true if, for instance, a nurse working for a group of doctors negligently injured a patient, or if a waiter working for a restaurant dropped a tray on a customer. In each case, the employer would be vicariously liable for the actions of its employee, even though the employer itself had done nothing wrong.

Why, asked Ellerth, shouldn't Burlington be vicariously liable for what its supervisor did to her, even if Burlington itself was not directly at fault?

Ellerth won—with some complications. The *Ellerth* case boiled down to two crucial rulings, each of which comprise a sea change in the law of the workplace.

First, the Supreme Court ruled that in cases where a supervisor sexually harasses an employee, and in the process takes some negative action against the employee (such as denying a raise or promotion), the company will he held liable, no matter what, even if the company actively prohibited sexual harassment, never knew that the sexual harassment was taking place, and did nothing else wrong.

Second, the Supreme Court ruled that even when no negative action is taken against the employee, if the employee is made to work in a sexually suggestive atmosphere that is unreasonably offensive—what the courts call a "hostile work environment"—the employer will be held liable, unless it can prove it did all it reasonably could to prevent and correct the harassment, and that the employee failed to take advantage of preventive or corrective opportunities the employer provided.

The Rules Have Changed

Ellerth's importance lies in its clear message to employers and employees: the rules of the workplace have changed, and are likely to change even more in the future.

As for employers, it is no longer enough to promulgate an anti-harassment policy, stick it in a personnel manual or post it in the lunchroom, and hope it works. Employers must proactively train and police their supervisory work-force and implement a zero-tolerance sexual harassment policy, coupled with real enforcement and real penalties. If they do not, they risk an avalanche of lawsuits to which they may have no defense.

As for employees, if they have been sexually harassed and their position in the company has been negatively impacted as a result, they win. Period. And if they are being victim-ized by a hostile work environment, and things don't improve even after they complain to their superiors and do their best to stop it, they win again. Period.

As for the future, *Ellerth* telegraphed a willingness on the part of the Supreme Court to expand the duty of employers to preempt not just sexual harassment, but any unlawful conduct directed at employees, and to expand the rights of employees to successfully sue their employers if their employers fail to measure up. Employees, be aware. Employers, beware.

22. STANDARD OIL CO. v. UNITED STATES

Eliminating Monopolies and Price Fixing: John D. Rockefeller and the Birth of the Antitrust Laws 1911

Think what things would be like if there were only one or two cell phone providers, pharmaceutical firms, or automobile companies. As things stand, you cannot watch television or read a magazine without being deluged with ads touting the superiority of one brand over another, and the price wars among competing companies can be fierce. But if there were only one or two companies in these fields, the incentive to innovate new and better products at cheaper prices would not be nearly as intense—and the consumer would suffer. Competition has always been viewed as a key to the free enterprise system.

"Antitrust law" is designed to preserve competition. The basic statutes were enacted by Congress in the late 1800s and early 1900s, but it was the Supreme Court that put flesh on the statutory bones, beginning in 1911 with the *Standard Oil Co. v. United States* case.

Restraints of Trade and the "Rule of Reason"

The Standard Oil Company was founded by John D. Rockefeller. Through a combination of ruthlessness and creativity, Rockefeller managed to combine the vast majority of the country's oil refining and distribution capacities under one roof, creating a classic monopoly. Having eliminated the competition, he could sell and charge what he wanted to whomever he wanted, and he did.

Spurred by muckraking journalists, the government ultimately took action and brought suit under the relatively new Sherman Antitrust Act to break up Standard Oil into separate, competitive businesses. The trial consumed weeks (the record includes some 14,000 pages of testimony) and the Supreme Court eventually agreed to render the final ruling.

In an undeniably landmark case, the Court broke up Standard Oil into separate, geographic units (not unlike what happened in the telephone industry decades later). In so doing, the Court announced a new rule to be applied in future monopoly cases—the so-called "rule of reason." The Sherman Act had prohibited *any* "restraint of trade," but the Supreme Court decided that only "unreasonable" restraints of trade (of which Standard Oil was the poster child) would be unlawful. In so doing, the Supreme Court gave birth to the federal government's power to analyze and, if warranted, seek the breakup of companies (as it attempted to do to Microsoft) and to minutely review and, if warranted, disallow proposed mergers that might restrain competition.

Price Fixing and "Per Se" Violations

Ever creative, companies in the early 1900s pursued another activity that allowed them to raise prices without creating monopolies: price fixing agreements. The leaders of competing companies in an industry would simply agree among themselves to maintain prices at an agreed-upon level, rather than trying to undercut one another. The usual effects of competition would be blunted, and the consumer would suffer.

Building on the *Standard Oil* precedent, in 1927, in the case of *United States v. Trenton Potteries Co.*, the Supreme Court ruled that price-fixing agreements among competitors are by definition an unreasonable restraint of trade, *whether or not* the levels at which prices were fixed were or were not reasonable. This became known as a "per se" violation of the antitrust laws, meaning that simply doing it is against the law, without regard for any "rule of reason." In the intervening decades, various other forms of collusion among ostensible competitors have been identified as per se violations as well.

Antitrust law has evolved into a huge body of court decisions, statutes, and regulations that permit both enforcement actions by the government and suits by private citizens and companies for antitrust violations. Scholarly debates among economists and politicians pertaining to the economic policies that should underlie the enforcement of the antitrust laws are ongoing, leading to different approaches taken by different administrations and different courts at different times. But when all is said and done, in the *Standard Oil* case the Supreme Court set forth the basics of some of the most important rules by which corporate America must live.

23. KELO V. CITY OF NEW LONDON
Can the Government Take Your House to Promote a Private Business? 2005

The concept of the government taking your house because it wants to use your property for some other purpose is frightening to contemplate. However, even before the Constitution was drafted in 1787, it was a given that a sovereign nation had this power of "eminent domain" or "condemnation." Our Founding Fathers recognized this in the Fifth Amendment to the Constitution, but restricted the right of the government to take private property (upon payment of just compensation) to one purpose: "public use."

Most citizens understand this as a necessary but limited evil that allows the government to take private property only in very rare circumstances, such as when a house lies in the path of a needed highway that will be used by the general public, or for a water treatment plant or similar public facility. Taking someone's home is not something a democracy that respects individual rights does unless absolutely necessary.

But can private property be lawfully taken in order to promote private business interests?

A Castle No More?

In 1997, Susette Kelo purchased and restored a home with a river view in the Fort Trumbull neighborhood in New London, Connecticut. Many other families lived in this older, middle-class neighborhood as well, some for many generations.

New London's economy had been faltering for some time and, in 1998, the pharmaceutical company Pfizer began building a major research facility next to the Fort Trumbull neighborhood. New London saw this as an opportunity for economic development and revitalization and, through a private development agency controlled by city government, it developed a plan to create jobs and increase tax revenues. The plan called for the purchase and demolition of the Fort Trumbull houses, after which private developers would build a resort hotel and conference center, research facilities, new homes, offices, and retail space where the Fort Trumbull houses had formerly stood.

New London began making deals to buy the properties in Fort Trumbull (there were 115 separate lots) for this purpose. When all was said and done, the owners of 15 lots, including Kelo, refused to sell. New London then commenced eminent domain proceedings in order to force the holdouts to sell their properties. In response, Kelo and the other holdouts sued to protect their homes, claiming that the proceedings would violate their constitutional rights. Eventually, the Supreme Court agreed to hear the case.

Kelo's argument was this: the Fifth Amendment says the government can take private property for "public use," but this land was not being taken for that purpose—it was being taken to build what amounted to a privately owned commercial real estate development in the hope of increasing tax revenues and spurring economic growth. The Founding Fathers had drawn a line, and New London had stepped over it.

"Public Use" Becomes "Public Purpose"

In 2005, by a very contentious 5-4 margin, the Supreme Court ruled against Kelo and in favor of New London. The Supreme Court decided that the meaning of the phrase "public use" in the Constitution also included projects pursued for a "public purpose." Granted, the Court said, the New London project would not be used by the public, like a highway or water plant, but the Fort Trumbull lots were being taken to benefit the public as part of a carefully considered, comprehensive economic rejuvenation plan that would serve the public's need for new jobs and increased tax revenue. For five of the nine justices, that "public purpose" was enough of a "public use" to satisfy the Fifth Amendment.

Justice O'Connor wrote a vigorous dissenting opinion. "The specter of condemnation hangs over all property," she wrote. "Nothing is to prevent the state from replacing any Motel 6 with a Ritz-Carlton, any home with a shopping mall, or any farm with a factory." She was particularly troubled by the potential for what the decision would mean to citizens who did not wield power among public officials. "The beneficiaries are likely to be those citizens with disproportionate influence and power in the political process, including large corporations and development firms," O'Connor wrote. "As for the victims, the government now has license to transfer property from those with fewer resources to those with more. The founders cannot have intended this perverse result."

Justice Thomas stated his dissenting view with equal force: "Something has gone seriously awry with this court's interpretation of the Constitution. Though citizens are safe from the government in their homes, the homes themselves are not."

The *Kelo* decision has been welcomed by state and local officials who have been struggling with economic redevelopment projects. At the same time, anti-*Kelo* forces are hard at work. Currently pending in the Senate is the Protection of Homes, Small Businesses, and Private Property Act of 2005 which, if passed, would prohibit use of the power of eminent domain for economic development projects. Similar bills have been introduced in the House, and in various states. Whether those statutes are constitutional may be on the Supreme Court's docket in the near future.

In the meantime, there is good news and bad news. The good news is that it will be easier for federal, state, and local governments to pursue economic revitalization projects. The bad news is that, as part of the process, your backyard may end up in the middle of a factory or hotel lobby.

24. MONROE v. PAPE
You Can Sue City Hall 1961

What happens when the government, which is responsible for creating the law, then violates the law? The Supreme Court sets limits on how far government can intrude into your life, but what are your rights if the government oversteps its boundaries?

As a practical matter, your right to hold the government accountable for its actions was uncertain and unpredictable, until the case of *Monroe v. Pape*. The *Monroe* case applies in a variety of contexts ranging from unlawful restrictions on businesses and property owners, to violations of the rights of criminal defendants. In any discussion concerning the boundaries of the government's power over businesses and individuals under the Due Process Clause, the Commerce Clause, or any other portion of the Constitution, *Monroe* answers the key question: what can those whose rights have been violated do about it?

In the *Monroe* case, thirteen Chicago police officers broke into Monroe's home in the early morning without a warrant, routed the occupants from bed, made them stand naked in the living room, and ransacked every room, emptying drawers and ripping mattress covers. Monroe was then taken to the police station, detained for ten hours while he was interrogated about a two-day-old murder without being permitted to call his family or attorney, and then released without criminal charges being brought against him.

Monroe sued the police officers for damages in federal court, under a post–Civil War statute generally referred to today as "Section 1983." Monroe chose this strategy, as opposed to filing a lawsuit in the local state court, because under state law his chances of successfully suing state officials or employees were slim, and he believed that local state court judges might be prone to protect local police officers. Section 1983, originally called "the Ku Klux Klan Act of 1871," was enacted by Congress to address the fact that many Southern states were refusing to protect freed blacks from whippings, lynchings, and other atrocities at the hands of whites, mainly Klan members. Monroe took the position that Section 1983 was more than an anachronism limited to the unusual circumstances of the post–Civil war era, and that it gave all persons whose constitutional rights were violated a federal right to sue for damages in federal court.

Using the Power of the Government Against the Governnment

Monroe v. Pape eventually reached the Supreme Court, and in a 1961 landmark ruling, Monroe won. The Supreme Court ruled that Section 1983 allowed individuals to bring federal court lawsuits for damages as the result of any "misuse of power" by state officials "clothed with the authority of state law." In 1971, the Supreme Court extended this ruling to allow claims in federal courts against not only state officials, but federal officials as well, in the case of *Bivens v. Six Unknown Named Agents of Federal Bureau of Narcotics.*

In the wake of *Monroe* and *Bivens*, literally thousands of Section 1983 cases have been succcessfully filed against government officials in federal courts for claimed violations of constitutional rights, such as actions based on unlawful searches, unlawful arrests, police brutatility, arbitrary regulation of business and property, improper taxation, governmental dishonesty, and much more.

At their core, the *Monroe* and *Bivens* decisions allow individuals whose constitutional rights have been violated to use the power of the government *against* the government—a remakable characteristic of our democracy that we have come to take for granted. This, in turn, has had a predictable effect on government accountability: faced with the prospect of having to explain their actions to a federal court jury, government officials become much more cautious before trifling with individual rights. For this reason, many commentators view *Monroe* and *Bivens* as being among the most significant decisions of the century.

Chapter 8
Limiting the Imperial Presidency

*"When the President does it, that means
that it is not illegal."*
—Richard M. Nixon

Those who have occupied the White House have frequently
tried to expand the scope of their authority and power.
Many have taken the position that the president is wholly
independent and has the right to do what he thinks best, without having to answer to the other branches of government.

When the framers of the Constitution, steeped in English
law, gathered in Philadelphia to debate and draft the
Constitution, they were familiar with such governmental
philosophies. For centuries, English law provided that "the
king can do no wrong," and untold generations suffered the
consequences of an unchecked monarchy. The English
emasculated that principle when they enacted the Magna
Carta in 1215, creating many of the fundamental rights
that eventually found their way into our Constitution. To be
sure, the framers had their disagreements over how
powerful the president should be, but no one held out for
the creation of an infallible monarchy—much, very much,
the opposite.

The fact that the president *can* do wrong, however, raises difficult questions about our system of checks and balances. Who decides if the president is wrong? How do you keep politics out of the process? What happens if national security is at stake? Not surprisingly, it has been, and will continue to be, the Supreme Court that answers these questions.

25. YOUNGSTOWN SHEET & TUBE CO. v. SAWYER

The Steel Seizure Sase: How Far Can the President Go in the Name of National Security? 1952

In June 1950, North Korea invaded South Korea, and the Korean War was on. As the conflict raged, the collective bargaining agreement between the United Steel Workers and the steel industry was due to expire, and the union demanded a substantial raise, which the steel industry refused. Attempts at settlement failed, and on April 4, 1952, the union gave notice of a nationwide steel strike to commence on April 9, 1952.

Steel was an indispensable component of the war effort, and President Truman believed that a work stoppage would jeopardize national security. Citing his authority under "the Constitution and laws of the United States, and as President of the United States and Commander in Chief of the Armed Forces," just a few hours before the strike was to begin Truman issued an executive order directing Secretary of Commerce Charles Sawyer to seize the steel mills from their owners. Truman explained his actions to the American people in a radio and television address, speaking of the grave dangers that would face the nation if the steel companies ceased production.

Less than an hour after Truman concluded his broadcast, attorneys for the steel companies appeared at the home of a federal trial court judge in Washington, DC, and requested an injunction prohibiting Truman's actions. They rightly pointed out that Congress had never passed a law authorizing a president to unilaterally seize control of an industry, no matter the circumstances, and they asked that their property be returned to them immediately. What, they asked, were the limits of the president's power?

The conflict gave rise to the case of *Youngstown Sheet & Tube Co. v. Sawyer*, better known as the "Steel Seizure Case." In the midst of blaring headlines and a rancorous national debate, it was once again left to the judiciary to write the rule book by which Congress and the president would be authorized to govern the country. The issues in the Steel Seizure Case were of such importance that the Supreme Court heard and decided the case just two months after the steel companies' lawyers appeared at the trial court judge's Washington home.

When the case got to the Supreme Court, Truman, through government lawyers, argued for the supremacy of the executive branch: in times of national emergency, the president has the power, and even the obligation, to step in and take action, and neither the Congress nor the judiciary has the constitutional right to stop him. Truman's argument did not depend on legal niceties. When there is a true crisis, he contended, a president must have the right to do what he thinks is right, without having to seek and wait for approval from the other branches of government.

The Supreme Court disagreed. After hearing two days of oral argument, it ruled against Truman by a 6-3 vote.

The "Zone of Twilight"

Justice Black wrote the majority opinion. He began with the foundational proposition that a president is not all-powerful, no matter the circumstances. A president cannot take action, said Justice Black, unless that action is authorized either by a statute passed by Congress, or the Constitution. Plainly, there was no statute authorizing a president to unilaterally seize private property (let alone an entire industry); whatever statutory authority there was protected private property from governmental seizure. The question, then, was whether the Constitution itself empowed Truman to seize the steel mills.

Truman's lawyers focused on Article II of the Constitution, which appoints the president as the "Commander in Chief." They contended that the commander in chief must have broad, expansive powers, as would a general on a battlefield. Justice Black, in terse language, rejected this argument, and ruled that the power of a "commander in chief" cannot extend so far as to allow the taking of private property in the name of national security. "This," he said, "is a job for the Nation's lawmakers, not its military authorities."

Justice Jackson, while concurring in the overall result, wrote a separate opinion which, over the years, has become much more influential than Justice Black's reasoning. Justice Jackson wrote that a president's powers are at their maximum when he seeks to enforce plainly expressed congressional will, and those powers are at their "lowest ebb" when he seeks to act against the will of Congress. But, he said, "there is a zone of twilight" between these extremes, and the limits of presidential power in these gray areas "is likely to depend on the imperatives of events"—that is, the president has some room to move in cases of true national emergency, so long as he does not directly violate the plainly expressed will of the Congress.

Justice Jackson concluded that Congress had in prior laws forbidden unilateral seizures of property, and for that

124

reason Truman's actions had to be overturned. But the implication was that if Congress had not plainly expressed its will on this very issue—that is, if Truman had been operating in the "zone of twilight"—Truman may well have been free to do as he thought best in view of the national security issues he faced. The message to both future members of Congress and future presidents was unmistakable.

Truman immediately complied with the Supreme Court's ruling. A fifty-three-day steel strike ensued, no steel shortage occurred, and a settlement was ultimately reached.

National Security Versus Civil Rights: The Beat Goes On

How far a president can go in the name of national security, and the extent to which Congress can rein in executive powers during such times, has always been and will remain a vital national issue of daunting complexity. There is, of course, no singular formula that can define the proper spheres of executive and congressional authority in all circumstances, particularly when, as is so often the case, the dispute resides in the "zone of twilight" described by Justice Jackson.

As recently as 2004, however, the Supreme Court again stressed that the president's powers are limited by law, even in wartime. Justice O'Connor, referencing the Steel Seizure Case, made quick work of President Bush's contention that he could hold suspected terrorists without a hearing. "We have long since made clear that a state of war is not a blank check for the president when it comes to the rights of the nation's citizens."

In 2005 and 2006, the Steel Seizure Case again took center stage during the Justice Alito confirmation hearings, and the Senate hearings on the Bush administration's domestic surveillance programs. Senator Specter stated at the commencement of the Alito hearing: "This hearing comes at a time of great national concern about the balance between civil rights and the President's national security authority." He went on to say, "The President's constitutional war powers as commander in chief to conduct electronic surveillance appear to conflict with congressional legislation in the Foreign Intelligence Surveillance Act. This conflict could activate the considerations raised in Justice Jackson's historic concurrence in the Youngstown Steel Seizure Case . . . It is a critical analysis for as Justice Jackson noted: 'What is at stake is the equilibrium established by our constitutional system.' "

The Steel Seizure Case continues to give Congress and the judiciary ample ammunition with which to challenge an exercise of presidential power that arguably oversteps legal boundaries. How such confrontations are resolved in the future will depend on an array of variables, such as whether the challenged presidential action impinges on individual civil liberties, whether it affects only foreign affairs or also domestic affairs, the immediacy and risks of the crisis at hand and, of course, the personal predilections, backgrounds, and philosophies of the justices who make up the Supreme Court at any given time.

26. UNITED STATES V. NIXON

*Nixon, Executive Privilege and the
Watergate Scandal 1974*

Can the president withhold information from Congress
merely because he is the president? Can the president over-
ride congressional efforts to oversee the legality of what he
does? The inglorious Watergate scandal ultimately forced
the Supreme Court to confront these issues in the most
dramatic constitutional crisis since the Civil War.

A "Third-Rate Burglary"

In June 1972, during the Nixon-McGovern presidential
campaign, five men with cameras and listening devices were
arrested inside the Democratic National Committee's
offices, located in the Watergate complex in Washington.
Thanks in large part to dogged investigative reporting by the
Washington Post (as portrayed in the book and movie, *All The
President's Men*), the burglars were publicly linked to Nixon's
reelection committee and administration officials. Despite
the administration's denials of any involvement (Nixon's press
secretary dismissed the break-in as "a third-rate burglary"),
public pressure mounted, and a Senate committee
conducted an investigation, followed by hearings in 1973.

The hearings were televised, and they captivated the
nation. As millions of citizens watched, various Nixon
administration officials, including John Dean, Nixon's
former counsel, claimed that Nixon's closest associates—
and perhaps Nixon himself—had orchestrated a cover-up of
the break-in and engaged in a host of other illegal activities.
Nixon was clearly in the Senate's sights: Senator Howard
Baker repeatedly asked witnesses the question that has

since worked its way into the nation's political lexicon: "What did the president know, and when did he know it?"

During an otherwise routine July 1973 hearing session, one of Nixon's assistants, Alexander Butterfield, revealed that Nixon had installed a taping system in the oval office, and had retained possession of the very tapes that would definitively and undeniably answer Senator Baker's famous question. Butterfield's revelation changed the nature of the Senate inquiry—why ask witnesses what Nixon was told and what Nixon said in the oval office when there existed the ultimate original source material, a tape recording?

The "Saturday Night Massacre"

By this time, honoring a promise he made during his Senate confirmation hearings, Attorney General Elliott Richardson had appointed Archibald Cox, a well-known lawyer, to serve as a special prosecutor investigating the Watergate case. Shortly after Butterfield's testimony, Cox served a subpoena on the White House, demanding the tapes. The battle was under way.

Nixon refused to produce the tapes, citing a murky legal doctrine known as "executive privilege." He contended that each branch of government was separate from the other, and legally entitled to be free from interference by the other. In fact, Nixon knew that, among many other embarrassments, the tapes included the "smoking gun," conversations in which Nixon sought to use the CIA to unlawfully obstruct the FBI's investigation of the Watergate burglary in the effort to hide the involvement of his administration and, perhaps, himself.

Nixon offered Cox a compromise involving a screening of the tapes by a Nixon senatorial ally and the production of edited versions. Cox refused.

The next night, October 23, 1973, a Saturday, Nixon ordered Attorney General Richardson to fire Cox. In view of the promise he had made to Congress, Richardson refused and, in protest, resigned. Nixon then ordered Deputy Attorney General Ruckelshaus to fire Cox. Ruckelshaus refused, and resigned as well. Nixon then ordered the Solicitor General, Robert Bork, to fire Cox. Bork was, by default, now in charge of the Justice Department and he, too, considered resigning. Bork, unlike Richardson, would not be violating a commitment to the Senate if he obeyed the order, and Richardson persuaded him to comply, for fear that the Justice Department would otherwise be thrown into turmoil. Bork reluctantly fired Cox, culminating what has been dubbed the "Saturday Night Massacre."

Congress was outraged, and various bills of impeachment were eventually introduced, charging the president with, among other things, abuses of power and obstruction of justice. The battle had escalated into a full-fledged war between Congress and the president.

The firing of Cox did Nixon no good, and lots of harm. Cox's successor, Leon Jaworski, doggedly pushed for the production of the tapes, and public pressure crescendoed. Nixon backpedalled, and released edited transcripts of the tapes. The transcripts corroborated much of what Dean and many witnesses had stated, but also included a very suspicious eighteen-minute gap, which Nixon blamed on his secretary, further fanning public cynicism and outrage.

Jaworski sought a court order compelling Nixon to obey the subpoena. Now all three branches of government were involved in the conflagration. Nixon again relied on "executive privilege," arguing that neither he nor any other president could fulfill the duties of the office if private conversations and planning sessions were subject to public disclosure. Nixon contended that he led a separate branch of government, and the other branches of government, Congress and the courts, had no right to compel him to take actions he felt to be unwarranted.

The lower courts entered orders, appeals were filed, and a major constitutional crisis loomed. It ultimately fell to the Supreme Court to define the boundaries of congressional, presidential and judicial power.

The Supreme Court's Decision: A President, Not a Monarch

It is now known that as they debated the case, the justices had substantial disagreements among themselves, but agreed that they *had* to speak with one voice. Nixon had publicly agreed to accept a "definitive" order from the Court, and the justices feared that if their opinion were not unanimous, Nixon would use that as a basis on which to defy the Court's order. This raised the specter of Congress and the Court sending federal marshals to remove the tapes from the White House, and the president, as commander in chief, mustering armed forces to guard the oval office. It was a risk the Court knew it could not take, and the justices managed to set aside their differences and reach a unanimous and clear result.

Chief Justice Burger announced the Court's decision on July 24, 1974: Nixon was ordered to surrender the tapes.

The Court recognized that a president could insist on a right to confidentiality in some circumstances, such as to protect national security—a concept later presidents have attempted to use when called upon to disclose their personal documents and records. Nixon, however, had not sought to avoid the subpoena on these grounds but, rather, claimed that executive privilege was *absolute*, that as the leader of an independent branch of government he could withhold what he wanted. Nixon's lawyer explained Nixon's position in his argument before the Supreme Court: "The President wants me to argue that he is as powerful a monarch as Louis XIV, only four years at a time, and is not subject to the processes of any court in the land except the court of impeachment."

The Supreme Court disagreed, ruling that a president is not above the law, and when faced with a subpoena issued to obtain evidence in an investigation of national importance with criminal implications, he must comply, as must any other citizen.

To his credit, Nixon complied less than a week later. The House Judiciary Committee had already begun impeachment proceedings, and Nixon knew that the evidence on the tapes would seal his fate. On August 8, 1974, reading the writing on the wall, Nixon resigned—the first president to do so. Vice President Ford assumed the presidency.

After being sworn in by Chief Justice Burger, President Ford announced that "our long national nightmare is over." As much as anything else, the "nightmare" was the prospect that the branches of government would defy each other, and that their disagreements could, literally, result in a confrontation of force. That did not happen, leading President Ford to emotionally, and correctly, observe, "Our Constitution works; our great Republic is a government of laws and not of men."

On September 8, 1974, Ford pardoned Nixon for any crimes he might have committed in the Watergate affair.

Chapter 9
How Free Is Free Speech?

"If liberty means anything at all, it means the right to tell people what they do not want to hear."
—George Orwell, British author and journalist

The First Amendment prohibits the government from "abridging the freedom of speech." It is difficult to overstate the importance of this precept to the Founding Fathers, and to our survival as a democracy.

But as the aphorism about yelling "Fire!" in a crowded theatre makes evident, free speech cannot always be so free. Speech, for instance, can take the form of calls to violence and anarchy, endangering entire communities. Speech can be obscene past the point of imagining and repugnant to the values that holds a society intact. Speech can endanger children.

Under-regulation of speech can be dangerous. Overregulation of speech can be more dangerous. It is the Supreme Court's unenviable job to determine where you draw the line.

27. BRANDENBURG v. OHIO
The Right to Be Repugnant 1969

In the 1960s, Clarence Brandenburg was a well-known leader of an Ohio Ku Klux Klan group. He invited a reporter to film various Klan activities, such as a cross burning attended by armed men. In the film, Brandenburg, in Klan regalia, made a speech threatening vengeance if the president, Congress, and Supreme Court "continues to suppress the white, Caucasian race . . . Brandenburg also advocated that blacks be transported to Africa and Jews be sent to Israel.

In the early 1900s, Ohio, like nineteen other states, enacted what was then known as a "criminal syndicalism" statute. Ohio's statute made it a crime to advocate "the duty, necessity, or propriety of crime, sabotage, violence, or unlawful methods of terrorism as a means of accomplishing industrial or political reform," and to assemble with a group for such purposes. After the film became public, Brandenburg was arrested and convicted under the Ohio statute, and sentenced to a fine and imprisonment.

Brandenburg challenged the constitutionality of the Ohio statute, claiming that it infringed on his basic First Amendment right to free speech. The Ohio courts turned down Brandenburg's appeal, and the Supreme Court then agreed to hear the case.

Only in America: The Right to Advocate Revolution

In its 1969 decision *Brandenburg v. Ohio*, the Supreme Court unanimously invalidated Brandenburg's conviction. The Court ruled that "mere advocacy" is free speech protected by the First Amendment and it cannot be punished—even when the speaker is advocating the use of force or the violation of law. Only advocacy that is "directed to inciting or producing imminent lawless action and is likely to incite or produce such action" can be restricted—what courts often call "fighting words." This is a crucial, constitutional line in the sand, and the Court ruled that any law or act of a government official that fails to appreciate this distinction "sweeps within its condemnation speech which our Constitution has immunized from governmental control."

Brandenburg exemplifies how far the Supreme Court will go to insulate speech from government interference, a perspective that carries over into many other arenas, such as the Court's reluctance to delve as deeply into the regulation of obscenity as many people feel it should. The decision stands as the Supreme Court's last word on the broad protections the First Amendment provides to speech that advocates force or lawlessness to effectuate social change.

Fundamentally, *Brandenburg* provides a constitutional safe haven for virtually all speech that communicates an idea or position, no matter how repugnant. Our traditions so respect the right of free speech that our government will protect even those who espouse that it be overthrown.

28. MILLER V. CALIFORNIA
Obscenity and the First Amendment 1973

One of the linchpins of a democratic society is this: people must know, clearly and in advance, what conduct can be prosecuted by the government as a crime, and what conduct is lawful. If the definitions are vague and blurry, the government can arrest whomever they don't like whenever they wish, and citizens must walk on eggshells for fear of recrimination, which is how dictatorships remain in power. Few scenarios could be more violative of the "government of laws, not men" envisioned by the Constitution.

"I Know It When I See It"

Decades ago, the Supreme Court ruled that "obscenity" is not protected by the First Amendment. What that meant as a practical matter was that the federal and state governments could make it a crime to distribute obscene materials, which is exactly what was happening. But how can "obscenity" be defined so that people might know, *clearly* and *in advance*, what they could do without risking a jail term? Without a clear definition, the local bookseller would risk a criminal record if he failed to remove from the shelves all of the novels with graphic love scenes (*Madame Bovary? Lolita? Ulysses?*), and the local theater would have to think twice before showing a movie with sexual content (*The Graduate?*). And what about the rights of adults to do what they want in their private lives without the government's "Big Brother" interference?

In a 1964 case, Justice Potter Stewart was asked to decide whether a movie under the Court's review was "hard core pornography," and he mirrored the maddening difficulty of trying to define what may be indefinable. "I shall not today attempt further to define the kinds of material I understand to be embraced within that shorthand description; and perhaps I could never succeed in intelligibly doing so," he said. "But I know it when I see it, and the motion picture involved in this case is not that."

The "I know it when I see it" test was not exactly the kind of standard that would provide fair notice of the activities that might land you in jail. But Justice Stewart's frustration was understandable: how can words draw clear lines between what is and is not obscene, any more than words can define what is and is not beautiful, or does or does not taste good?

"Movie Day" in the Supreme Court

The upshot of a rule that says you can only know obscenity when you see obscenity is that, eventually, you have look at obscenity—and through the 1960s that's just what the Supreme Court justices did.

According to various articles and books about the Supreme Court (often based on accounts from former Supreme Court law clerks), many of the justices and their clerks regularly gathered in the Supreme Court basement on what came to be known as "movie days" to review films that were the subject of obscenity prosecutions. Some justices refused to participate. Others took it as a solemn duty. But a few seemed to enjoy their work. Justice Marshall, it was said, sat in the front row and joked loudly, even asking for copies of films so he could show his children when they were older. Justice Harlan, who was nearly blind, mischievously sat next to more prudish colleagues and insisted that they narrate the on-screen goings on, to his great amusement ("Oh, extraordinary!" he would frequently exclaim).

By the early 1970s, the Supreme Court was ready to find a different solution.

Let Someone Else Do It

In 1973, the Supreme Court again tackled the obscenity issue in the case of *Miller v. California*, which continues to represent the last, definitive word on the subject—at least to the extent a 5-4 decision can be "definitive."

Miller was convicted under a California obscenity statute for knowingly selling brochures that displayed men and women engaged in sexual activity. The law at the time stemmed from a 1957 case, *Roth v. United States*. Under *Roth*, in order to be obscene, a court had to find that the "dominant theme taken as a whole appeals to the prurient interest" of the "average person, applying contemporary community standards." Later cases added that only materials that are "patently offensive" and "utterly without redeeming social value" could be obscene.

By 1970, two of the sitting justices, Douglas and Black, believed the First Amendment protected all speech, including obscenity, and Justice Brennan, who had written the *Roth* opinion, had concluded that efforts at definition were fruitless and counterproductive. Chief Justice Burger, however, believed that a framework should be developed that permitted localities to create their own obscenity standards, and he politicked among the justices for a majority vote in favor of that position.

What emerged from an extremely contentious debate among the justices was a bare majority in favor of a three-part test that would define what could be prosecuted as "obscenity":

(a) whether the average person, applying contemporary community standards would find that the work, taken as a whole, appeals to the prurient interest,
(b) whether the work depicts or describes, in a patently offensive way, sexual conduct specifically defined by the applicable state law, and
(c) whether the work, taken as a whole, lacks serious literary, artistic, political, or scientific value.

If all three criteria were met, the work could be considered obscene, and those who distributed it could be charged with a crime.

In effect, the Supreme Court, while setting some definitional limits, abdicated responsibility for defining obscenity. The upshot of *Miller* was to permit each locality to impose its own definition. What a jury in one locality might consider "prurient" might be considered "literature" in another.

Justice Stewart would no longer be able to know it when he saw it; it would depend on where he was at the time.

Making Obscenity a Federal Case: The New Wave of Prosecutions

The Miller decision resulted in literally hundreds of obscenity prosecutions in the few years after the case was decided, until the dust settled and the rules of the game in each community became better known. For many years thereafter, obscenity cases were rare.

That all changed in 2000, when the Bush administration began bringing federal obscenity prosecutions. By way of comparison, there were four obscenity prosecutions during the eight years of the Clinton administration. Between 2001 and mid-2005, the Bush administration obtained more than forty obscenity convictions, and numerous indictments are pending. Given Miller's focus on community standards, the prosecutions were most often brought in communities believed to be more traditionally conservative, making the prospect of obtaining a conviction more likely. In December 2005, for instance, a Florida man was sentenced to five years in prison by a federal judge in Montana for distributing obscene video tapes throughout the country.

Where all this leaves the obscenity issue may become extremely interesting in the near future. Given the important First Amendment questions that obscenity questions raise, one or more of the Bush adminstration's obscenity prosecutions could easily find their way to the Supreme Court.

Senators, congressmen and the media consistently speak of the "conservative" tilt of the Supreme Court in recent years, particularly in view of recent appointments. But the "conservative" label has a different meaning when applied to a Supreme Court justice than it does when used in a political context. A "conservative" politician is often understood as one who favors more "traditional" values, and would seek to prohibit the distribution of sexually explicit materials. A "conservative" jurist, however, is typically regarded as one who takes laws in general, and the Constitution in particular, more literally, without attempting to inject personal values or notions of social justice.

The First Amendment says that the government "shall make no law . . . abridging the freedom of speech." It does not say that the government may make *some* laws. *No* law. We may soon see just how "conservative" the Supreme Court really is.

———◦◦◦———

29. TEXAS V. JOHNSON

The Flag Burning Case:
Can Conduct Be "Free speech"? 1989

The First Amendment protects "freedom of speech," but people often communicate and express themselves in nonverbal ways. For that reason, the Supreme Court has, for many years, recognized that conduct, like gestures or demonstrations, can have a communicative element, and can be "speech" for First Amendment purposes. For instance, the Supreme Court has ruled that when, in the context of a political protest, a student wears a black armband to school in violation of school rules, the student is plainly attempting to communicate an idea, and the armband is "speech" entitled to First Amendment protection.

But how about burning the American flag? Just how far does the First Amendment go?

During the 1984 Republican National Convention in Dallas, Gregory Lee Johnson participated in a demonstration against the Reagan administration and its policies. The demonstration culminated at Dallas City Hall, where Johnson unfurled an American flag, doused it with kerosene, and set it on fire while others chanted, "America, the red, white and blue, we spit on you." No one was injured or threatened, but many were seriously offended.

Johnson was arrested and convicted under a Texas statute, similar to statutes in forty-seven other states, prohibiting the desecration of the flag. He appealed his conviction, and the Supreme Court agreed to hear his case in 1989.

Johnson contended that the Texas statute violated his First Amendment rights of free speech. Johnson argued that what he did was not just an act of meaningless destruction, but was clearly meant to convey a political message protected by the First Amendment.

Texas argued that flag burning cannot be construed as "speech," but even if it were, not all "speech" is protected. The Supreme Court had long ago ruled that speech intended to incite imminent violence or other public harm does not merit First Amendment protection. Texas argued that flag desecration fell within this exception to the First Amendment: the flag represented the nation itself and, consequently, the desecration of the flag was so offensive to so many people that it *always* involved the threat of violence.

Can Setting a Fire Be "Speech"?

By a bare 5-4 majority, the Supreme Court agreed with Johnson, and ruled the Texas statute unconstitutional. Justice Brennan wrote, "If there is a bedrock principle underlying the First Amendment, it is that the Government may not prohibit the expression of an idea simply because society finds the idea itself offensive or disagreeable." He concluded that preserving the fundamental right of freedom of expression, no matter how repugnant that expression may be, was more important than preserving the flag as a symbol of nationhood.

The dissenters were livid. Flag burning is not "speech," Chief Justice Rehnquist wrote, but rather "is the equivalent of an inarticulate grunt or roar" whose only purpose is "not to express any particular idea, but to antagonize others." Johnson was punished not for his ideas, said the dissenters, but for committing an act that is regarded as profoundly repulsive to the majority of citizens—and just as society has the right to legislate against offensive conduct like embezzlement and pollution, it has the right to legislate against flag burning.

The *Texas v. Johnson* decision provoked the House and Senate to pass condemnatory resolutions, and President Bush supported a constitutional amendment outlawing flag desecration. Others in Congress supported an anti–flag burning statute. Those forces prevailed, resulting in the Flag Protection Act of 1989. Almost immediately, that law was challenged, and the Supreme Court ruled it to be unconstitutional on the same bases expressed in the *Texas v. Johnson* decision. Since that time, there have been repeated calls for a constitutional amendment but, to date, proponents have been unable to garner sufficient votes in the House and Senate to force the issue.

As for the line between conduct that is regarded as speech and protected under the First Amendment, and conduct that does not implicate the First Amendment, it is interesting to compare the Supreme Court's 1968 decision in *United States v. O'Brien*. In that case, O'Brien burned his draft card during an anti-war protest, and he was arrested under a federal law making the intentional destruction of a draft card a federal crime. O'Brien's draft card burning was, plainly, the same kind of political protest as Johnson's flag burning, but this time the Supreme Court let the conviction stand. The difference, according to the Court, was that Congress had a legitimate interest in the preservation of draft cards in order to assure the efficient operation of the selective service system. So, while that element of O'Brien's conduct that was "speech" might be constitutionally protected, there was another element to his conduct that was not "speech" and could be punished.

30. NEW YORK TIMES CO. V. SULLIVAN

The Freedom to Criticize Public Officials and Public Figures 1964

Although the First Amendment protects "free speech," not everything that is said or written is defined as "speech" worthy of a First Amendment shield. Some examples have been discussed previously, like "fighting words" intended to incite immediate violence, or obscenity. Another example stems from the centuries-old common law of defamation: you cannot falsely call someone a thief or an incompetent in public, and then hide behind the First Amendment when you're sued for the damage you did to their reputation. Defamation law covers both false statements made in writing (libel) and false statements made in spoken form (slander). Either way, the law recognizes the right we all have to protect our good names.

At the same time, however, our democracy, like any democracy, depends on the ability of citizens to speak freely about their public officials without fear of reprisal. This is the essence of the First Amendment, and one of the key freedoms that distinguishes us from a dictatorship. But here's the difficult part: what happens if, in the course of speaking out about a public official, you inadvertently say something that turns out to be false? For instance, based on information you got from the town bookkeeper, you honestly think that the tax collector is embezzling tax money, and you say so at a public meeting. The tax collector is fired and his reputation is ruined. It turns out, however, that the bookkeeper was wrong, but you didn't know that at the time.

You certainly had a First Amendment right to speak out, but don't public officials have the right to protect their reputations, like anyone else? And if they do have the right to sue for libel and slander, what effect will that have on the willingness of citizens to freely speak their minds about important issues at the next public meeting?

In 1960, a group seeking, among other things, to raise funds for the legal defense of Martin Luther King Jr. ran a full page ad in the *New York Times*. The ad included statements that the Montgomery, Alabama, police had engaged in serious acts of misconduct. As it turned out, the statements were false. L. B. Sullivan, the city official who oversaw the police department, brought a libel action against the *New York Times*, and a local jury awarded him the then unprecedented sum of $500,000.

Is There a Right to Lie?

The *New York Times* appealed, claiming that the case violated crucial rights of free speech, and the Supreme Court agreed to hear the case. The issue was how the country should balance the First Amendment right to speak out about their public officials, against the right of those public officials to protect their reputations from false statements. In its decision, the Supreme Court spoke very clearly about which way that balance should tilt.

Justice Brennan wrote the Court's majority opinion. He began by stating the obvious: "Freedom of expression upon public questions is secured by the First Amendment." But he then went a remarkable step further and ruled that, contrary to the entrenched principles of defamation law, even false statements about public officials would from that time forward be protected by the First Amendment. Justice

Brennan wanted to make sure that citizens could speak out about their public officials without having to look over their shoulders. As he put it, even false statements must be protected if this basic right of public discourse is to have the "breathing space" it needs to survive.

But Justice Brennan also set limits: only false statements made about public officials *in good faith* would be protected. No protection would be given to a false statement made with "malice"—that is, with the knowledge that it is false or, very important, with "reckless disregard" of whether it is false.

The *New York Times Co. v. Sullivan* limitation on defamation suits by public officials was extended in later cases to also include "public figures"—movie stars, people frequently in the media, and so on. The logic is that when you are in the public spotlight, the public should have a First Amendment right to talk about you in good faith, without fear of lawsuits.

The Real-World Impact of *New York Times Co.* v. Sullivan

Picture a campaign for governor between Sam Smith and John Jones. Smith hires an investigator. The investigator tells Smith that he has evidence documenting that Jones uses cocaine. Smith immediately starts running attack ads, calling Jones "the Cocaine Candidate." Jones loses the election and his reputation is ruined. It turns out that the investigator's information was false—the drug user was a different John Jones, not the candidate. Jones sues Smith for libel. Smith defends by claiming that he placed the ads in good faith, based on the information provided by a professional investigator, and that under the First Amendment, candidates in an election campaign are allowed to make mistakes. What more could he do?

Jones, however, wants to know whether Smith showed "reckless disregard" for whether or not the reports were false. As Justice Brennan explained, if Smith recklessly disregarded the truth, Smith could be liable to Jones. Did you make sure the investigator corroborated the sources? Did you personally interview any of the people who made the accusation? "John Jones" is a common name; did you do *anything* to make sure this was not a case of mistaken identity? Or did you just put on blinders because you *wanted* the information to be true?

The "reckless disregard" issue is the battleground on which these cases are usually fought. It is tough to prove that someone intentionally lied, and the question usually boils down to whether they cared enough about the truth to seek it out. Remember, in order to be liable for defamation of a public official, it takes more than just a disregard for whether a statement is false—it takes a *reckless* disregard, which is a much higher standard.

New York Times Co. v. Sullivan is there when a national news anchor reports a story on congressional misconduct; or when a local newspaper reporter attempts to expose a municipal conflict of interest; or when a citizen comes to a town meeting to complain that the mayor drinks too much; or when a business journal critiques the performance of a famous CEO; or when an Internet blog asserts that a rock star was lip-synching during a recent concert. It continues to define our rights of public discourse.

31. NEW YORK TIMES CO. v. UNITED STATES

The Pentagon Papers Case: Balancing National Security Against the People's Right to Know 1971

What happens when a reporter obtains information about an important national issue of great interest to the American people, but the government believes that disclosure of the information would harm national security? Does national security trump a journalist's (or anyone else's) First Amendment right of free speech? If it does, how is it to be determined if the government's national security concerns are genuine, or are really excuses to avoid political embarrassment?

In 1967, Secretary of Defense Robert S. McNamara commissioned a classified study to disentangle how the United States became involved in the Vietnam War. The report took more than a year to complete, and encompassed forty-seven volumes, with extensive documentary evidence. Later dubbed the "Pentagon Papers," it included evidence that the government lied to and misled the American people, and that various presidents had overstepped their lawful powers.

Daniel Ellsberg was a Cambridge- and Harvard-educated economist who served in the military, consulted with the government on key issues such as the Cuban missile crisis and, having been identified as a rising intellectual resource, was asked to join the Defense Department in 1964 to work for McNamara. In this role, Ellsburg visited Vietnam, and observed what he believed were substantial flaws in the development and implementation of United States policy. Ellsburg began to morph from an enthusiastic hawk to a very cynical dove.

From 1967 to 1969, Ellsburg, at McNamara's request, helped to compile the Pentagon Papers, and in the process Ellsburg further confirmed what he saw as rampant governmental deception and misconduct. At the height of his disillusionment, Ellsburg copied substantial portions of the Pentagon Papers and provided them to the press.

The *New York Times* began publishing excerpts from the Pentagon Papers, and the Nixon administration immediately filed a lawsuit, claiming that national security would be compromised if publication continued. Government lawyers successfully obtained an injunction to stop further publication—the first time the government had sought an injunction to stop a newspaper from publishing the news. The *New York Times* appealed to the Supreme Court, but in the interim, the *Washington Post* obtained a copy and began publication, resulting in another government lawsuit; the *Boston Globe* then began publication as well. The Supreme Court, recognizing the serious issues involved, expedited the usual procedures, immediately scheduled oral arguments and just four days later issued its ruling.

Can The President Edit the Evening News?

Decades before, the Supreme Court had ruled that the First Amendment does not permit courts to order a "prior restraint" of free speech, except in the most unusual circumstances. In other words, courts can award damages if what is said or written constitutes libel or slander, and courts can send someone to jail if what is said or written constitutes a crime, but courts cannot, except in the most extraordinary cases, issue orders prohibiting the act of speaking or writing itself.

Owing to the speed with which the case found its way to the Court, the justices issued a joint, very brief opinion reiterating the law regarding prior restraints of speech, stating that the Nixon administration had "a heavy burden of showing justification" for the restraint on the publication of the Pentagon Papers, and concluding that it had not met that burden. The Pentagon Papers were published, and they fueled widespread and accelerating opposition to the Vietnam war, as well as increasing cynicism about government in general.

In addition to this brief statement, several justices of the Court used the case to publish their own lengthy and detailed opinions in which they expressed their views on freedom of the press, and in which they excoriated the government's attempt to stop the publication.

Some justices took the position, consistent with the rulings in some prior cases, that if the publication of certain information would clearly create a direct, immediate, and irreparable injury to the nation, a prior restraint could be issued. Those justices concurred in lifting the injunction against the Pentagon Papers, however, because they felt that the government had not come close to such a showing in the case before the Court.

Other justices, notably Justice Black and Justice Douglas, took the position that the government may *never* keep information from the public. Justice Black wrote, "In my view it is unfortunate that some of my Brethren are apparently willing to hold that the publication of news may sometimes be enjoined. Such a holding would make a shambles of the

First Amendment." He went on to describe the role the Founding Fathers envisioned for the press. "The press was to serve the governed, not the governors. The Government's power to censor the press was abolished so that the press would remain forever free to censure the Government. . . . In revealing the workings of government that led to the Vietnam war, the newspapers nobly did precisely that which the Founders hoped and trusted they would do."

Freedom of the Press in a Post-9/11 World

In a post-9/11 world, the conflict between national security and the public's right to know, as exemplified by the Pentagon Papers case, has been heightened. This conflict raises many of the most difficult issues democracies face, and compelling arguments can be made in support of a variety of policy positions. The *New York Times*, for instance, was blessed by some and cursed by others for its exposure in 2005 of the government's previously secret program of domestic electronic eavesdropping, and a multitude of approaches has been suggested by congressmen, senators, and commentators of all parties and political leanings.

However the executive and legislative branches may choose to address these issues in the future, it is unlikely that their decisions will be the last word. The magnificence of a system of government like ours is this: when it works like it's supposed to work, whether the public's right to know has been properly respected by its elected officials is ultimately measured against the requirements of a Constitution that transcends whatever policy preferences may exist at any point in time. And the measuring is to be done by Supreme Court justices with no axe to grind other than the preservation of the core values of the Constitution itself.

Chapter Ten
Old Laws and New Technologies

"Invention is the mother of necessity."
—Thorstein Veblen, economist
and political commentator

The cotton gin and the steam engine helped change an agricultural society into an industrial society. Mega-factories and a national economy soon followed, and families, workplaces, and governments were forever transformed. In response, a whole new body of laws emerged to address the never-imagined problems new technologies always bring with them. This is how jurisprudence evolves: with each new brainchild, there is always a need for new laws to help resolve new issues.

Yet the Constitution, an eighteenth-century document, remains the fundamental law of our land. How can it apply to twenty-first-century issues? Can an eighteenth-century prohibition against unreasonable searches be sensibly enforced against a twenty-first-century police force? Does the eighteenth-century concept of "free speech" have meaning to the twenty-first-century Internet?

And what happens if the Constitution turns out to be an ancient round peg that simply will not fit within a modern square hole?

32. MGM STUDIOS INC. V. GROKSTER, LTD.

Music, Movies, and the Internet 2005

Grokster, Ltd. was in the business of distributing free software that allows computer users to share and copy electronic files on a "peer-to-peer" basis—that is, directly from one computer to another computer without having to go through a central server. The Grokster software could be used to share any kind of computer file, but as Grokster well knew, the software was primarily used as a tool to infringe on copyrights—millions of times a month, Grokster users sent copyrighted materials to each other, such as music and video files. The effect was, basically, a high-tech, geometrically multiplied version of what would happen if one person buys a book and then makes thousands of copies and gives them away for free, in violation of the author's copyright.

To increase its user base, Grokster actively promoted its software as an easy and efficient way to exchange copyrighted music and video files, and even offered instructions to users who called the Grokster help line. Grokster was not paid by its users, but as the number of users increased, Grokster could generate more advertising revenue.

MGM (along with a group of other copyright holders) sued Grokster for copyright infringement. MGM sought an injunction to stop the use of the Grokster software, and also sought damages from Grokster for the copyright infringements committed by the computer users to whom Grokster distributed its software.

The "Guns Don't Kill People" Defense

Grokster had some solid defenses—and it won in the lower courts. There was no evidence that Grokster itself ever infringed on a copyright, and it was not contested that, for instance, students and business executives who wanted an efficient way to exchange word processing files or spreadsheets could and did use Grokster for completely legal purposes. Grokster contended that it could not be held responsible if users chose to employ its software for illegal purposes—the technological equivalent of the "guns don't kill people, people kill people" defense.

In fact, there was substantial legal precedent for Grokster's position. There was no basis in copyright law for holding someone liable for creating a product that others used to infringe copyrights. When Sony introduced its VCR, for example, movie studios sued, claiming they would be ruined because VCR users could unlawfully record and copy movies instead of going to theaters. The Supreme Court eventually heard the case, and ruled in favor of Sony. Yes, VCRs could be used to unlawfully copy movies, said the Court. But they were also capable of lawful use, and Sony could not be held responsible for the fact that some users might use them improperly.

When *MGM v. Grokster* got to the Supreme Court, Grokster made the same argument about its software that Sony made about its VCR—but unlike Sony, Grokster lost. What was the difference?

In the *Grokster* case, the Supreme Court faced a situation in which it had to find a way to do *something*. If copyright protection means anything, owners of copyrighted materials, like music and video files, had to have a way to stop the blatant infringement that the peer-to-peer software enabled. In the past, copyright owners could sue those doing the infringing, but in the peer-to-peer world it was almost impossible to track down who was sending what computer file to whom. Billions of dollars were being lost.

Yet, copyright law, as demonstrated by the Sony precedent, provided MGM with no rights against Grokster, since Grokster was not the one doing the infringing.

A Government of Men, and Not Laws?

Grokster is an excellent example of what happens when courts, armed only with laws rooted in the eighteenth century, confront twenty-first century technology issues that the lawmakers never could have foreseen, and that the laws were never meant to address. In reaching its decision, the Supreme Court exercised its supremacy, and did what it so frequently does when faced with such situations: it found a way to change the law so it could do what it felt had to be done.

The Supreme Court decided that even though Grokster made a product that, like the VCR, could be used for lawful purposes, Grokster had "induced" its customers to use its product for unlawful purposes, and Grokster should be held liable for that unlawful inducement. It was as if Grokster sold an electric screwdriver, but advertised and supported it as a means to pick locks and commit burglaries. The Supreme Court made it clear that "mere knowledge" of the fact that a product was being used unlawfully would not be enough to create liability. Sony, for instance, knew that some customers used VCRs unlawfully. But Sony marketed VCRs as a device to be used for lawful purposes, such as "time shifting" —recording a program so it could be viewed at another time. Grokster, on the other hand, energetically encouraged its users to take a product that could be used lawfully, and use it unlawfully; that was the difference between being liable, and not being liable.

MGM v. Grokster will most certainly change the way Americans share music, video, and other copyrighted materials over the Internet. A concern raised by many commentators is whether it will also have a chilling effect on the development of new technologies that could be used for either lawful or unlawful purposes. The jury is (almost literally) still out on that fear. Apple originally marketed the iPod through its "rip, mix and burn" slogan—an apparent invitation to copyright infringement—but has nevertheless won the approval of the recording industry. Portable hard drives that fit inside a wallet are perfect for copying MP3 music files from a friend's computer, but there is no apparent movement to ban these devices. The difference seems to lie in the fact that these products can be used primarily for lawful purposes, and the manufacturers are not, overtly or behind the scenes, promoting their use for unlawful purposes.

But what about the way in which this new body of law was created? A company like Grokster might convincingly argue that by departing from precedent in this way, the Supreme Court unfairly changed the rules in the middle of the game. What happened to the "government of laws, not men" concept? Didn't Grokster's owners, when they invested in the company, have a right to rely on the law as it was written at the time?

There are no easy answers. Ultimately, the law's job is to reflect society's views on what is fair and just. When faced with conduct that, while technically legal, violates society's sensibilities, the Supreme Court must make the difficult of choice of mechanically applying the law as it exists, or tweaking the law so that the results comport with established notions of justice. The Supreme Court often chooses the latter alternative: individuals and companies inevitably find the unforeseen cracks and loopholes in the law, and if the Supreme Court thinks the result is more than society should be required to tolerate, it does what it needs to do to seal the cracks and close the loopholes.

33. KYLLO V. UNITED STATES

How Much Privacy Are You Entitled to in a High-Tech World? 2001

Unlike the implied right of privacy on which the *Griswold* and *Roe* cases discussed previously were based, there is an explicit right of privacy plainly expressed in the Fourth Amendment to the Constitution. That provision restricts the right of the government to snoop into the personal affairs of Americans through the admonition that the "right of the people to be secure in their persons, houses, papers, and effects, against unreasonable searches and seizures, shall not be violated." If the government wants to conduct a search, the Fourth Amendment mandates that it must go to a judge and obtain a warrant "upon probable cause, supported by Oath or affirmation, and particularly describing the place to be searched and the persons or things to be seized."

But how much privacy does the Fourth Amendment actually provide in a high-tech world, where the FBI and even the local police have electronic devices and computer capabilities that can do what the framers of the Constitution could not possibly have imagined?

Federal agents were suspicious that Danny Lee Kyllo was growing marijuana in his home. The agents secretly set up a thermal-imaging device outside the Kyllo home in order to determine if the heat emanating from the home was consistent with the high-intensity lamps typically used to nurture indoor marijuana plants. The scan showed that Kyllo's garage roof and a side wall were relatively hot compared to the rest of his home and were substantially warmer than neighboring homes. On the basis of that information, the agents obtained a warrant, searched Kyllo's home, found growing marijuana plants, and convicted Kyllo on a federal drug charge.

Kyllo argued that his conviction should be overturned because the government's use of the thermal-imaging device to detect what was going on inside his house was "an unreasonable search and seizure" that violated his rights under the Fourth Amendment. Still, how could that be? All the government did was monitor what was going on *outside* of Kyllo's house.

Can You "Search" a House Without Ever Going Inside?

Over many years, the Supreme Court has developed a body of rules that flesh out the meaning of the Fourth Amendment. At their core, these rules mandate that citizens are entitled to privacy within their homes, and that the only way the police can invade that privacy is by going to a judge, demonstrating the need to invade that privacy, and obtaining a warrant. There are some limited exceptions, such as true emergencies. But other than that, our homes are our castles, and the government's right to intrude into our homes requires a warrant.

Kyllo's situation presented another example of what happens when eighteenth-century laws meet twenty-first-century technology. What happens if, using the latest electronic and computer capabilities, the authorities can look inside your home without ever getting close to your front door, and without you even knowing they are in the neighborhood? Does the Fourth Amendment prohibit the government from analyzing what is happening outside of a house in order to determine what is going on inside the house?

Kyllo lost his case in the lower courts, and the Supreme Court agreed to hear his appeal. Most commentators believe that since at least the 1990s, the Supreme Court has favored law enforcement authorities, and in the process has relaxed many of the rights afforded to those who commit or are accused of committing crimes. Therefore, the presumption was that Kyllo's argument would be viewed with disdain, and that the Supreme Court would use the case as a means to put another arrow in law enforcement's quiver.

Privacy Trumps Technology

It did not turn out that way. Kyllo won. In the process, the Supreme Court began the effort to set limits on "Big Brother" that will help to further define twenty-first century privacy rights.

The Supreme Court ruled that unless the government gets a warrant, it cannot use a device that is not in general public use to effectively look inside a private home from the outside: if the police would need a warrant to go into the house to find out what was going on inside, they must get a warrant to accomplish the same result using high-tech devices from outside the house. In years past, the Supreme Court had ruled that the government can, without a warrant, use binoculars to look through the windows of a house (or even fly overhead) to see what is in plain view. But the *Kyllo* Court ruled that other than that, citizens have the right to expect what's inside of their homes to remain private, and that right of privacy is violated just as much by a police officer crawling through a window as it is by the use of technology to accomplish the same result. The message was clear: if the police want to see what's not in plain view inside a private home, they need a warrant.

There are a myriad of technology versus privacy issues that the Supreme Court has not yet had the opportunity to address, and *Kyllo* may be a key indicator of the direction in which the Supreme Court will head. For instance, reportedly, the government has developed a technology it calls "Magic Lantern," through which it can email a program to a suspect's computer and then monitor the suspect's computer keystrokes. Isn't this a way to peer inside a home from outside the home, and wouldn't the logic of *Kyllo* require overenthusiastic government agents to first obtain a warrant?

What about homeowners who use wireless computer networks? Wireless network signals can be picked up from outside a home. Could local police who think you may be conducting illegal activities in your house set up on the public street outside your home, tap into your wireless network, monitor your emails, and search your hard drive?

In *Kyllo*, the Court stated its intent to protect fundamental rights against the end runs that new technologies can provide to government authorities. For citizens concerned about their rights of privacy, *Kyllo* is a first step in an important direction. An issue the Court will no doubt face in the future is whether deviations from that path should be permitted in the face of emerging law enforcement challenges and national security issues.

34. UNITED STATES v. AMERICAN LIBRARY ASSOCIATION

The Internet, Free Speech, and the First Amendment 2003

The First Amendment's prohibition of laws "abridging the freedom of speech" is among our most cherished rights. As shown in some of the cases discussed previously, our traditions hold that free speech is a linchpin of democracy. Once government gets into the business of deciding what kinds of speech or written materials are appropriate, a very dangerous line has been crossed. Whatever social ills may result from allowing tasteless or repugnant expression is a price you pay for freedom.

But What About the Kids?

But consider this situation. To assist your thirteen-year-old son with his schoolwork, you buy him a notebook computer and arrange for a high-speed connection to the Internet. Later, you find out that he has been accessing pornographic websites. You can install filtering software on his computer, but those programs are anything but perfect; they can be expensive and, besides, he's always going to have access to the Internet when he visits his friends. The Founding Fathers never envisioned anything like the Internet. Isn't there room in the First Amendment to protect children from Internet content they simply should not see?

In 1997, in the first Internet-related Supreme Court case, *Reno v. American Civil Liberties Union*, the Supreme Court considered the constitutionality of the federal Communications Decency Act (CDA). The CDA prohibited the transmission of any "indecent" or "patently offensive" messages or displays to a minor, or in a manner that is available to a minor. The question was whether the CDA violated the First Amendment, and the Supreme Court ruled that it did.

The Supreme Court reasoned that the Internet was a unique "marketplace of ideas," and for the good of our democracy, it was entitled to the same, broad First Amendment protections as books and other publications. The government was simply not entitled to "chill" free expression, even if that expression might be offensive to some, and yet the CDA would have precisely that effect. How would those persons responsible for websites dealing with, for instance, birth control practices, or homosexuality, or the legal issues involved in pornography know in advance if a court would ultimately find their materials to be "indecent" or "patently offensive," and how would they keep minors from accessing their materials without also barring access to adults? While it might be true that software could be devised so that websites could tag and filter potentially offensive content in a way that only adults could access, the Court decided that adults should not have to jump through technical hoops to read and view what they wanted.

The Court's ultimate conclusion was this: while minors need to be protected, that protection cannot be implemented in a way that burdens and compromises the First Amendment rights of adults, and the CDA, however laudable its purpose, went too far.

Now picture a situation in which you drop off your teenager at the local public library to do some research. After you leave, he heads for the library computer terminals and accesses websites that include pornographic materials.

The library knows that kids might use its computers for this purpose. Shouldn't it block access to these sites?

But, on the other side of that coin, what about the First Amendment rights of adults who use those same computers to view whatever they want in a publicly funded library, free from government interference? Isn't a library the one place where you should be able to read anything you want without someone looking over your shoulder?

The Supreme Court confronted these questions in 2003, in the case of *United States v. American Library Association.* The case involved a challenge by the American Library Association to the constitutionality of a congressional statute that, for the purpose of protecting children, denied federal funding to libraries that refused to install filtering software that blocked obscene materials on all library computers.

The system envisioned by the statute would allow adults to have librarians unblock the computers while they were using them. But the reality was that adults would often be too embarrassed to make the request, fearing that they would be perceived as seeking to view pornography in the library when, in fact, that was not the case: the filtering software did not work very well and was a serious impediment to normal adult usage of the computers for research or casual reading. As a result, one justice wrote that, contrary to the very purpose of the First Amendment, the statute "prohibits reading without official consent." The American Library Association sued, it said, to protect what libraries are supposed to be.

Surprisingly to many, despite its decision in the Reno case, the Supreme Court ruled against the American Library Association's position and upheld the constitutionality of

164

the statute. It concluded that so long as the library staff would freely unblock the filters without delay, the importance of protecting children outweighed the (theoretically) small burden on adult First Amendment rights occasioned by the requirement that they approach a librarian and ask for permission to read and view what they want. The implication of the ruling is that if, in practice, specific libraries fail to quickly accede to adult requests, those libraries may be required to remove the filters (and lose funding), but that was a bridge to be crossed later.

Defining the Future of the Internet

The *American Library Association* case is an important, some say scary chink in the First Amendment armor in which the *Reno* case had cloaked the traditionally free-wheeling, anything-goes Internet. The issue is whether the case will be limited to its specific facts, or whether it signals a trend away from *Reno*, toward what many see as the slippery slope of Internet censorship. Given, for instance, the ubiquity of computer access minors have in today's world, why shouldn't filters be required on *all* computers? And what if it turns out to be impractical to protect children from inappropriate Internet content through filtering devices that can be turned on and off? In the interest of protecting children, should Congress then attempt to regulate Internet content itself? And if it makes sense to regulate Internet content, what about blogs and emails? But if that's the tactic used, who will decide what Internet content should be filtered or restricted, and on what basis will those decisions be made?

There is no denying the breathtaking difficulty of such issues, and the Supreme Court seems to be signaling that it is ready to enter the fray. For instance, in 1998, in response to the *Reno* decision, Congress enacted the Child Online Protection Act (COPA). Like the CDA, COPA imposed fines and imprisonment for posting material "harmful to minors" on the World Wide Web, but it attempted to address the issues that caused the Supreme Court to find the CDA unconstitutional. COPA was, nevertheless, quickly ruled unconstitutional by lower courts, and after years of procedural wrangling the Supreme Court agreed, ruling in 2004 that COPA created the "potential for extraordinary harm and a serious chill upon protected speech."

But very significantly, rather than striking COPA from the statute books as it almost always does when it finds a law to be unconstitutional, the Supreme Court sent the case back to the lower court with orders that the lower court investigate whether the latest content-filtering technology could be used to achieve COPA's objectives within the constraints of the First Amendment. Rather than shying away from the issue, the Supreme Court is actively seeking to confront it.

On parallel tracks, interests groups are readying test cases highlighting the innumerable other intersections between the First Amendment and the Internet. The results of these cases will define much of the face and function of the Internet itself, and the effect of those precedents will ripple in unforeseeable ways through the myriad other technologies and innovations that so dominate our society.

Afterword

Our goal must be to remain the "government of laws, not men" that our Founding Fathers envisioned. But for so long as men have the power to change the laws, achieving that goal will require persistent vigilance.

Democracy American-Style

Here's the way it's supposed to work. Democracy American-style means that government—Congress, the president, or the local town council—can do what they think best concerning the laws they enact and the actions they take. But, all the while, they know that the Supreme Court lurks in the background, reserving the right to sound the alarm if constitutional boundaries are violated. In this way, our system deters and defeats those who would seek to convert our government of laws into a government of men who substitute their own judgments and interests for our fundamental constitutional freedoms and guarantees. The Supreme Court serves as the Constitution's whistleblower.

Great theory . . . except, as the foregoing chapters have hopefully made plain, the Supreme Court is itself made up of men who may seek to substitute their own views for the Constitution's mandates, and even when acting in the utmost good faith, their actions are colored by their own foibles, backgrounds, and opinions. The Supreme Court has the power to police the constitutional compliance of the executive and the legislature, but who polices the Supreme Court?

167

Given the Supreme Court's power, it can be disconcerting to admit, as we must, that Supreme Court justices, like all humans, are fallible. Moreover, even the most supreme of justices, like all humans, see the world through the lens of the events and norms of their times. Many of the Supreme Court cases discussed previously make this all too plain. The Fourteenth Amendment, for instance, assures "equal protection" and, indeed, "Equal Justice Under Law" is literally carved in stone over the entrance to the Supreme Court itself. Yet for decades, highly respected Supreme Court justices consistently deemed "separate but equal" racial segregation constitutionally acceptable. That precept was ultimately reversed, but it was not reversed because the words in the Constitution changed. It was reversed because different justices raised in a different era and informed by different social values knew it to be wrong—but it took fifty years to happen.

How can a country, let alone a judicial system, function when that which the highest court in the land finds to be a constitutional certainty on one day becomes a constitutional anachronism on the next?

"The Worst Form of Government . . ."

Yet when the array of checks, balances, and interrelationships is dispassionately analyzed, the most remarkable part is this: despite its undeniable failures and foibles, our system works better than the Constitution's framers could have hoped.

The reason for this success lies not just in the design of the system; it also lies in the qualifications and integrity of the people who have served within the system. The axiomatic lesson to be drawn from that reality must never be ignored or forgotten.

The vast majority of those selected to serve on the Supreme Court have been men and women of utmost good faith and open mind who, despite their differences in judicial philosophy and life views, treated the Constitution with awestruck reverence. In addition, the Court has produced a pantheon of social and judicial thinkers of extraordinary wisdom—Holmes, Cardozo, Brandeis, Frankfurter, and many more—who perceived the system's weaknesses and pitfalls, and skillfully navigated the country around and through them. The inherent fluidity of the law has only rarely been used to promote personal agendas, and has instead served as a self-correcting mechanism that allows the law to adjust over time to emerging realities.

The result has been the creation of an astounding body of law that has both reflected, and directed, the changing social and cultural landscape of our country. Justice Oliver Wendell Holmes Jr. put it best. "The life of the law," he said, "has not been logic; it has been experience." The way in which the Supreme Court has utilized the experiences of the country, and itself, to channel the law and, in turn, the way we live and function, is astonishing.

Clearly, there is room for substantial disagreement over the wisdom of many Supreme Court decisions. It has often taken much too long for injustices to be remedied. In hindsight it is plain that serious, sometimes damaging errors have been made. But when the whole of the Supreme Court's two centuries of work is reviewed and assessed, it is difficult not to be enthralled. It has become a cliché to remark, as did Winston Churchill, that "democracy is the worst form of government except for all those others that have been tried." In this country, the Supreme Court can take much pride in the cliché's continuing life as a demonstrable truth.

Inventing the Future

Today's Supreme Court faces daunting issues that have as much to do with philosophy, ethics, politics, and economics as with legal interpretations. Depending on how activist an approach the Supreme Court chooses to undertake, it can literally redefine the workings of government, the responsibilities of business, the place of religion, the nature of the family, and a host of other issues that will determine how Americans live and work.

The Court has already agreed to again review the way in which political campaigns are financed, and how the boundary lines of congressional voting districts are drawn. These decisions have the potential to change the nature of the Congress, as well as the presidency. It has also agreed to decide the constitutionality of restrictions on partial-birth abortions, and other limitations on *Roe v. Wade*. The Court will determine whether workers can recover damages from companies that employ lower-paid illegal aliens, and in the process it may set the tone for how the country deals with its borders. The balance between the powers of the presidency and concerns for civil liberties will likely be addressed, and it will be the Court that defines the limits of what a president can do in the name of national security. Whether schools will be permitted to teach "intelligent design" is headed for the Court. Whether, and how, Internet content will be restricted in the interests of protecting children is an issue plainly on the horizon. The extent to which

Congress can intrude into local business and government will garner additional Court attention. The constitutionality of funding faith-based service organizations with public funds is being challenged. The right of gays to marry and to receive the same state and federal benefits that are afforded to married couples is being pushed toward the Court.

The Supreme Court has defined much of our past. We now live in an era in which the Supreme Court is, in fundamental ways, inventing our future.

No governmental institution is better suited to the task.

Resources

If you would like more information about the Supreme Court, the case histories, and constitutional law, I recommend the following reference material:

CASEBOOKS AND TREATISES

These books are typically used in university or law school courses. They provide a very detailed and scholarly explanation, analysis, and critique of the Supreme Court's most important constitutional decisions.

Barker, Lucius J., Twiley W. Barker, Jr., Michael W. Combs, Kevin L. Lyles, and H.W. Perry Jr. *Civil Liberties and the Constitution*. 8th edition. Englewood Cliffs, NJ: Prentice Hall, 1999.

Cushman, Robert E., and Brian Stuart Koukoutchos. *Cases in Constitutional Law*. 9th edition. Englewood Cliffs, NJ: Prentice Hall, 2000.

Epstein, Lee, and Thomas G. Walker. *Constitutional Law for a Changing America: Institutional Powers and Constraints*. 5th edition. Washington: CQ Press, 2004.

Fisher, Louis. *American Constitutional Law* 5th edition. Durham, NC: Carolina Academic Press, 2003.

Ivers, Gregg. *American Constitutional Law: Power and Politics*. Boston: Houghton Mifflin, 2001.

O'Brien, David M. *Constitutional Law and Politics*. 5th edition. New York: W.W. Norton & Company, 2002.

Rossum, Ralph A., and G. Alan Tarr. *American Constitutional Law*. 6th edition. Belmont, CA: Wadsworth/Thomson Learning, 2003.

Stone, Geoffrey R., Cass R. Sunstein, and Louis Michael Seidman. *Constitutional Law*. New York: Aspen Publishers, Inc. 2005.

Tribe, Laurence H., *American Constitutional Law*. 3d edition. Eagan, MN: Foundation Press (Thomson-West), 2000.

GENERAL INTEREST BOOKS

These books are written for non-lawyers interested in the Supreme Court, its body of work, and how the Constitution is (or should be) interpreted.

Breyer, Stephen G. *Active Liberty: Interpreting Our Democratic Constitution*. New York: Knopf, 2005. The views of Justice Breyer, a sitting justice on the Supreme Court, concerning his philosophy of how the Constitution should be interpreted and applied to modern situations and issues.)

Hall, Kermit L. *The Oxford Guide to United States Supreme Court Decisions*. New York: Oxford University Press, 2001. A detailed compilation and summary of Supreme Court decisions.

Irons, Peter, *A People's History of the Supreme Court*. New York: Penguin, 2000. An analysis of the Supreme Court's decisions in the context of their times and the political environments in which they were decided.

Rehnquist, William H. *The Supreme Court*. New York: Knopf, 2001. The former chief justice's explanation of the significance and logic of key Supreme Court cases, with insights into the behind-the-scenes politics and influences that often swayed the Court's decisions.

Scalia, Antonin. *A Matter of Interpretation: Federal Courts and the Law.* Princeton: Princeton University Press, 1998. The views of Justice Scalia, a sitting justice on the Supreme Court, concerning how courts in general, and the Supreme Court in particular, should interpret and apply the Constitution and other laws. Justice Scalia's views are significantly different than those expressed by Justice Breyer in his book, and the differences illuminate why so many Supreme Court cases are decided 5-4.

WEBSITES

These websites provide a wealth of current and historical information about the Supreme Court, as well as access to searchable databases which include the Court's opinions, briefs submitted by the litigants, and audiotapes of the oral arguments made in some of the most famous and important Supreme Court cases.

http://supct.law.cornell.edu/supct/context.html Cornell Law School, Legal Information Institute, Supreme Court Collection. An excellent source of information about the Supreme Court, with easy access to current cases, and six hundred of the Court's most important decisions.

http://www.gpoaccess.gov/constitution/browse.html A service of the U.S. Government Printing Office. Provides an annotated explanation of each provision of the Constitution, with citations and links to important Supreme Court cases. http://www.oyez.org/oyez/frontpage Includes not only information on pending and recent Supreme Court decisions, but also hundreds of hours of actual audiotapes from oral arguments presented in famous Supreme Court cases.

http://www.supremecourtus.gov/ The official website of the Supreme Court. Includes information about the Court, pending cases, recent opinions, as well as other features, such as copies of briefs submitted by the litigants.

About the Author

Michael G. Trachtman is a founder and president of Powell, Trachtman, Logan, Carrle & Lombardo, P.C., a litigation and business practice law firm located in suburban Philadelphia, and a founder and CEO of Counsel Consulting Group, LLC, a national consulting and management training firm that assists companies seeking to avoid employment practices liabilities and related problems. He is the author of *What Every Executive Better Know About the Law* (Simon & Schuster), which focuses on the avoidance of business difficulties through the application of preventive law principles, and has written numerous articles published by business and professional organizations. He lives, with his wife and son, in Chester County, Pennsylvania.